Winning a Generation Without the Law

Essentials of the Gospel for a Postmodern Culture

Bryan Fraser

Winning a Generation Without the Law
by Bryan Fraser

Printed in the United States of America

ISBN 9781609573997

Unless otherwise indicated, Bible quotations are taken from the New King James Version. Copyright © 1982 by Thomas Nelson, Inc.

www.xulonpress.com

How lonely sits the city
   That was full of people!
   How like a widow is she,
   Who was great among the nations!
                Lamentations

Author's note:

In deciding whether to use the label 'Christian' or 'Evangelical' in this book, I faced the question, "Just what does one call a theologically conservative follower of Jesus in the 21st century?" While 'Evangelical' has had a lengthy tenure in this role, it has endured a tumultuous semantic ride in the last decade, most recently being abducted by network election reporting, wherein it is increasingly pressed into service to identify a voting bloc rather than a theological position.

In the hope of avoiding any such political connotation, I opted for the terms 'Christian' and 'Christianity' to describe that community holding to the historic, orthodox faith that confesses the divine inspiration and authority of the Scriptures and the necessity of personal faith in Jesus Christ unto eternal life. I admit in advance that I have drawn this circle so as to exclude some who would claim to be inside it.

Preface

Christianity has two distinct and separate mandates: to commend the law to those who have the Holy Spirit and to declare the gospel—stripped of all that is not the gospel—to those who do not. This book's basic premise is that Christianity has a long history of mingling these two streams inappropriately. The tragic result is that, after centuries of bending under the burden of a law it could not keep, Western society has finally reached its tipping point. In the space of a single generation, our postmodern culture has disowned its traditional theistic heritage, stormed out of the house in a huff and is presently living at no fixed legal address.

In the aftermath of this messy divorce, Christianity now directs its most fervent rhetoric not *to* the community of faith, but *against* those outside it. Any campaign against contemporary culture that rallies the troops to stand firm against the lawless hordes will quickly attract a loyal following of the disgruntled faithful who are fed up with society's "no boundaries, no rules" mantra and just aren't going to take it any more. However, many of the battles that seem so intuitively right and morally satisfying serve only to protest the passing of a bygone era beyond recovery. They do not build Christ's kingdom today.

This brief study examines 21st-century Christianity's penchant for taking up battles the gospel doesn't need fought—and the resulting alienation of society. I offer my thoughts on ten battles waged on the wrong hills of the postmodern landscape; battles popular spirituality too easily assumes to be essential elements of the gospel, but which actually connect very poorly with a lawless generation. Christianity insists on seeing society's departure from the law as a rejection of Christ, when the root problem is its own failure to interpret the gospel to a culture without the law.

The "cold war" mentality Christian culture presently maintains toward secular culture does not reflect either God's will or his purpose in dispersing his messengers of the gospel into the world. I will argue instead that Christians are to avoid rather than pursue conflict against those without the law. It is my hope that readers of this book will gain some understanding of why these battles are counterproductive, discover a few surprises and, ultimately—realize that they have permission to cease hostilities.

Haida Gwaii, British Columbia
June 2010

Table of Contents

Prologue:
A Time of Discomfort

To fight and conquer in all our battles is not supreme excellence; supreme excellence consists in breaking the enemy's resistance without fighting.

Sun Tzu

I hadn't planned to stop for lunch this early, certainly not along this funky downtown boulevard. My thoughts drifted back to how quaint and comfortable this neighborhood was when I grew up here. My parents long ago sold out and most of my childhood friends were out in the suburbs now. My sudden appetite surprised me. Despite a hearty breakfast, I felt that I would faint if I didn't eat immediately. I spotted a deli ahead on the next block with the name, "THE ENCHANTED MUSHROOM" hand-carved on a wooden sign.

I signaled and pulled over, hardly believing what I was doing. Before I knew it, I found myself inside the door.

I gingerly parted the curtain of hanging beads as I walked tentatively into the entryway. I paused briefly to glance at a bulletin board overrun with posters promoting meditation workshops, manifestos boycotting products of unclean corporations, notices of rallies condemning some impending political injustice, and ads seeking genderless roommates. After my eyes adjusted to the dim lighting, I saw that today's specials were scrawled in various pastel colors on a chalkboard. The list featured assorted organic dishes I couldn't pronounce, a vegan stir fry, roasted tofu on a bed of quinoa, fair-trade coffee drinks and the like. Middle Eastern tapestries and tie-dyed fabrics decorated the walls. Some pungent smoke of dubious origin floated lightly in the air. Being well before the lunch hour, there was only a sparse scattering of customers. None of them seemed to be in any hurry to finish their business and rush off.

The dining room was set one step down from the entry alcove. It was as I descended this step that I immediately became aware of an indescribably refreshing atmosphere in the restaurant. The sense of well-being, contentment and satisfaction that washed over me was nothing short of palpable. It was as if my soul and every physical sense agreed as one that this was the best place I could ever be. Whatever influence this was lifted my spirit to a level above every form of fear, worry, sorrow and weariness. I was dumbfounded. I couldn't reconcile this grungy café with my overwhelming euphoria.

A stranger was eating at a table in the corner when I walked in. Looking back at events now, I recall that my very first impression of him was that he was definitely a stranger. Of course, I felt quite out of place in this restaurant myself. From that perspective, I suppose I was a stranger as well. However, this man was clearly from...well, from someplace else. At the time, it was very difficult to express just what I sensed about him or how I knew that that he was from somewhere very foreign.

I chose a table that was not too close to his, but still close enough where I could observe him without obviously staring at him. Or did I choose the table? From the moment I walked into the dining room, it seemed that I was being drawn to this table rather than choosing it. I walked deliberately to the place where I was supposed to sit. It was the location prepared for me and I had no idea how I knew that. A waitress displaying the requisite inventory of tattoos, body-piercing jewelry and thrift-store peasant wear brought me a menu. She greeted me with a warm smile and told me that she would be back in a minute to take my order.

My seat faced the stranger directly. He was facing obliquely from me at an angle of 45°. This allowed me to study him without him realizing I was doing so—or so I imagined. In terms of his overall appearance, there was nothing particularly distinctive or remarkable about him. His clothes were so exceedingly generic that their very plainness marked him as a foreigner, but I could not associate his dress with any particular culture or locale. His hair was medium length, just touching the top of his back collar. Yet here was where I noticed the first truly unusual thing about him that I could articulate. I could not tell what color his hair was! This was not a trick of the restaurant's lighting, but an actual phenomenon of its appearance. It was is if his hair only reflected light so as to reveal its texture, but absorbed all the light waves that would indicate its color. As hard as I strained my mind to identify a particular hair color, my eyes simply couldn't register one.

Having paused at this visual mystery, I also noticed that his skin had much the same property. Was he tanned or pale? Was his skin tone white, black, Asian, Native American or middle Eastern? I just couldn't tell. Furthermore, his skin had neither the suppleness of youth nor the weathering of old age. His was a timeless countenance that concealed both his age and any clues to his ethnicity.

Of one thing there was no doubt: the stranger's bearing confirmed that he had seen much and was a man of considerable experience and wisdom. I pride myself on my ability to read a person by his appearance and manner. Is he a professional, an academic or a tradesman? Is he from the city or the country? Is he formally educated or self-taught; conservative or liberal? Does he pursue seclusion or social interaction? Has his life followed a path of pain and heartbreak or satisfaction and success? The stranger was all of these things and yet limited by none of them. I was convinced that he had the capacity to walk each of these paths and do so genuinely. Finally, his whole demeanor exuded trustworthiness and openness.

The stranger finished his meal, shaking me out of my mesmerized contemplation. He placed his napkin and silverware on his plate and started to rise from his seat. At no time during my appraisal of the stranger did I see him glance toward me or show any awareness of my interest in him. I chided myself for the flight of imagination I had allowed myself. In a moment, he would walk past me out of the restaurant and I would never see him again. I would reflect on this unusual encounter for a day or two and then it would blend into the flow of a thousand other demands on my attention and fade from memory.

But the inevitable thing was not what happened at all. The stranger walked directly to my table and sat down opposite me without any apology or introduction. It was the last thing I expected, yet the most natural course of events once he was sitting at my table talking to me.

"I've looked forward to speaking with you very much. I have important matters to discuss with you. Afterward, you must convey what I tell you to many others so that they will understand the times that are upon them."

Amazing as it may seem, his statement, made without any prelude or explanation, did not seem the least bit unusual or unexpected. This table, in this smoky coffee house, listening to this stranger draw me into his purposes was exactly where I was supposed to be. I answered him easily and naturally, without any trepidation. I answered him using the only response I could have summoned in such a situation. It only occurred to me later that another man in a desert spoke these same words long ago:

"Here I am, Lord."

* * *

I have always found casual conversation with very distinguished or accomplished people strained, feeling a self-imposed pressure to sound intelligent or to impress. My conversation with Jesus that afternoon was entirely free of this awkwardness. I would have pictured myself sitting across the table from him with his eyes drilling right through me, probing all kinds of dark and hidden secrets. Our talk was not that way at all. In fact, it was the most normal and relaxed conversation of my life. Certainly it was not an exchange of ideas between equals. Yet, there was not a hint of condescension or paternalism toward me as he unfolded his thoughts to me and patiently entertained my questions.

He began matter-of-factly, neither hurried nor in any way uncertain about the flow of his discourse. He paused in reflection occasionally, but I think this was to allow me to absorb what I was hearing rather than for his own benefit.

"Much has changed and will continue to change in the West. I have brought my people into a period of testing where they face many unfamiliar challenges. This turmoil is necessary because their old ways will no longer accomplish my purposes in the coming days. My people must interpret these times by my Spirit rather than with their own eyes. When I first built my church under the Roman Empire, I sent my people out as sheep among ravenous wolves, warning them to be wise as serpents and harmless as doves. From this position of weakness and vulnerability, they accomplished great and marvelous works. Today my people have become more like the wolf pack itself, using its tremendous strength and cunning to surround and take down its prey. You must tell my people that the times of the wolf are ended. My Spirit will not bless such conduct."

"I have removed my people's lampstand from the places of honor and influence in this society. In the coming times, my people must accept their place in an increasingly secularized culture. Their former influence in education, law, politics and social order is ended. I have brought these things to pass. My people must once again become as sheep and not as wolves."

"But I don't understand, Lord," I protested. "How can it be that you have done these things? Why would you turn society against yourself?

"I haven't turned society against me. I had to cut it loose from a religious spirit that has increasingly distanced itself from my voice. This culture hasn't rebelled against me. It has rebelled against a yoke of illegitimate authority that it would no longer bear. Don't assume that all the lawlessness of this age is directed at me. True rebellion against my Spirit is much more insidious and is deeply hidden in people's hearts. It is not openly visible."

"My people have lost their way. I sent them into the world to accomplish one task: to testify of me and to proclaim the life that I offer to those who thirst and hunger. Some will embrace the life that comes through me and many will not. My people have forgotten this, although I foretold it plainly when I walked among you."

"The Spirit has come into the world to do an entirely different work which my people can never do: draw people to me. He is the one who will convict the world of sin, and of righteousness, and of judgment. My people today have usurped the role of my Spirit. They have taken upon themselves the task of conviction. But my people cannot do the work of the Spirit. When they try, the result is rebellion, resentment and great hardening of hearts. They cannot change people's minds until my Spirit changes their hearts. My people no longer trust my Spirit to accomplish his work in the world. They refuse to rely on him to do the real work for which my Father sent him. Instead, they try to force the people of the land into my house by coercion. I could not bear it any longer, so I have brought my people into a time of discomfort where they must learn again many old truths long forgotten."

"I have cast a great blindness on the people of the land. I have made them as children, no longer able to discern good from evil, truth from error or wisdom from folly. They can no longer think or hear or see according to the wisdom of their fathers. In doing this, I have made my own people strangers in the land. I have placed my people in a culture so foreign and alien that they will be forced to abandon their weapons of flesh and blood. All this was necessary so that my people will return to my ways and once again rely on my Spirit to draw to me those whom I have called."

In my own readings of the gospel stories, I had always scoffed at the dullness of the disciples as they stumbled in confusion over Jesus' teachings. Now it was my turn to have my own dullness exposed and I understood their struggles at last. As Jesus unfolded these things to me I was losing my bearings. So much that I had viewed as certain and solid was crumbling as he spoke to me.

"This is incredible to me, Lord. You mean to say that **you** have actually brought about this disintegration of Western culture over the last generation? But we have fought so hard against this revolution! We have taken our stand for you and resisted the rebellion that has taken over our society."

"Rebellion takes many forms. Yes, I am grieved at the misery and confusion of the West. I wish it did not have to be so. But my people have not responded according to my Father's heart. And in their domineering attitude is also much rebellion. I had to remove their influence and status in society, for these were corrupted and beyond recovery. They have made too many unholy alliances with the kings of the land. They invoked my name too often in the pursuit of their own security, comfort and dominance. My people have taken up many battles that are not my battles. These efforts have the appearance of righteousness, but they only serve to satisfy the appetites of the flesh and do not advance my kingdom. And so I have humbled my people and have removed the honor and respect they once received from the people of the land. This is the message that you must deliver to my people. You must tell them that they will endure a time of humiliation, but that they will emerge with new hearts and a new vision for the people of the land. My people have grown hearts of stone, but I will give them hearts of flesh and they will look upon their brother and sisters with compassion once more."

"But, Lord, how will I do this?" I asked. "What will I say?"

"I will show you the way and tell you what you must say. Do not worry about the reaction you receive. I have prepared those who will respond to your message and those who will lead my people into this new time. Remember the old things that you learned long ago: that I can accomplish my purposes through many or through few."

Jesus paused for a second as a broad smile spread across his face. "Do you know what caused the peace and euphoria you felt when you came in here?"

"Why no," I flustered. "I meant to ask you what..." I stopped in mid-sentence as the reality hit me. "It's you, isn't it? It's because you're here!"

"That's right," Jesus confessed. "It's my aroma. It's the most powerful influence my people have in this world, and yet the most neglected. This restaurant had no esteem in your eyes, though many here yearn to meet me. You judged it according to the law, but I did not come to judge. My presence drew you here. You could not resist me, even though your mind fought to overrule your spirit. In the times ahead, my people will learn to rely on my aroma once again and will lay down their weapons of flesh and blood. The people of the land will come into my good pasture seeking refreshment and they will be satisfied."

Jesus laid his hand on mine and I felt his strength course through my body. The doubt and uncertainty I felt a moment before dissipated instantly.

"Tell my people that I am always with them and that no purpose of mine will ever fail."

With that parting encouragement, Jesus rose from his seat and walked past me toward the door. For a moment, I couldn't move, trying to somehow take in everything I had just heard. I then managed to gather myself and turn around, wondering if I might offer some fitting farewell. However, he was already gone and I saw no further sign of him.

As I turned back to the table, my eyes swept across the dining room and I took in a scene I could hardly process—the room was packed with customers and not a seat was available anywhere. The restaurant had completely filled up during our conversation and I had not been aware of it at all until this moment. Not only that, but the crowd was buzzing with a vibrancy that defied explanation— smiling, laughing and conversing among different tables. Just then, the waitress returned, clearly frazzled by the sudden rush of customers.

"I've never seen anything like this here before! Would you like to order now?"

As I glanced over the menu, I realized that I was completely out my element. I seemed to go blank for a moment, but finally managed to mumble a response.

"What do you recommend?"

1. The Battle of the Past

The Battle of the Past is Christianity's struggle to restore the 20th-century culture that was under the law.

> *Do not say, "Why were the former days better than these?" For you do not inquire wisely concerning this.*
> *Ecclesiastes*

Christianity has staggered into the 21st century with the blank stare of someone blindsided by divorce papers in the afternoon mail. As it prepares to inaugurate its third millennium, Christianity finds that its equity in Western culture has nearly vanished in a single generation. Without warning, society has told Christianity to clean out its desk and be escorted out of the building within the hour. Where Christianity was once society's trusted physician, confessor, advisor, vice principal and 24-hour plumber; it is now regarded as the senile great uncle, expected to sit quietly in the corner at family gatherings and not say anything embarrassing. Pluralism, naturalism, secularism and humanism now define the consciousness of the Western democracies. Forty years after the counter-culture revolution, a new generation has risen up that "knew not Joseph" and is hardly aware that such a revolution even occurred! A postmodern society is the only world the new generation has ever known.

This current worldview has transformed the theological, ethical and philosophical baselines of Western society with the silent efficiency of a stage crew changing sets between acts of a play. The Judeo-Christian assumptions that formed society's legal and moral fabric forty years ago are now popularly relegated to the derogatory categorizations of 'ultra-conservative,' 'extreme right wing' or 'fundamentalist' ideology. Traditional Christian thought now huddles in a walled-city mentality, doing its best to repair the breaches from the last enemy attack while preparing for the next onslaught. This "circling of the wagons" even takes on a geographic aspect, with certain communities and regions emerging as Bible-belt "safe" zones.

This crisis has brought 21st-century Christianity to a crossroads where it faces the decision of which role it will now pursue: the one it inherited in the 1st century or the one it claimed in the 20th. Christianity's present situation displays points of similarity with both of these eras. On the one hand, Christianity now faces an environment of religious and philosophical plurality, just as it did in the 1st century when it was a vulnerable, persecuted splinter sect, uncertain of survival in the polytheistic world of the Roman Empire. On the other hand, 21st-century Christianity is not the fledgling, ragtag upstart it was in the 1st century. It still retains much of the strength acquired in the modern era when it became a powerful cultural and political empire in its own right.

What is unprecedented about Christianity's present position in the West today is that, even while officially banished from the arena of public discourse, it remains a powerful, though increasingly isolated player in the social order. The Democratic Party underestimated the capacity of Christianity to unleash its moral weight in 2004 with the result that George W. Bush was able to secure a second term in the White House. (One can evict the elephant from the zoo, but one can hardly ignore the fact that it continues to stomp around outside the wall, trampling the flowers and uprooting trees.) 1st-century Christianity could not escape the constraints it faced under Rome. It was politically and socially powerless and it had no choice in the matter. However, 21st-century Christianity has a very real choice as to whether it will continue in the role of the elephant or look to a different model. The level of alarm and consternation involved in making this choice is understandable, for a single, generation has lived through both the former and present times. So it was when the temple of Jerusalem was rebuilt, that "many of the priests and Levites and heads of the fathers' houses, old men who had seen the first temple, wept with a loud voice when the foundation of this temple was laid before their eyes."

This book is about how Christians can make this choice and how their decisions will determine which battles they fight in this strange new postmodern world. I will argue that the model of a visibly activist, culturally-dominant Christianity is not practical, necessary, biblical or even possible. I will advocate a role for Christianity in the 21st-century that recalls its incredible expansion during its first 100 years; a period in which it had no access to the legal and political power echelons of Rome. Historian Philip Schaff explains this success, pointing out that, "Christianity reformed society from the bottom, and built upwards until it reached the middle and higher classes, and at last the emperor himself." We easily lose sight of the fact that 21st-century culture contains all the ingredients that produced the most productive period of growth Christianity has seen. We can no longer afford such an oversight.

A contrary view to my position is that Christianity's rightful mandate is to focus all of its remaining influence into restoring the worldviews of the 20th, the 19th, (or even the 16th) centuries; that Christianity must somehow push back the incoming tide of postmodernism as a necessary precursor to preaching the gospel. Champions of this approach assert that Christianity must first wrestle postmodern culture back into a traditional orientation under the law before it can go about its real business of evangelism. They would argue that Christianity cannot properly do its work until it is nested in a culture that already has a theistic paradigm as its predominant worldview. Some Christians even believe this struggle against postmodernism *is* evangelism!

In order to appreciate the futility of undertaking such a crusade, it behoves Christianity to consider how complete and radical the transformation of the 21st-century mindset has been. Postmodernism is somewhat difficult to define precisely because its basic premise is the non-existence of fixed categories and boundaries. Essentially, it is the belief that all traditional values, religious moral standards and Western political/economic structures derive from outdated, patriarchal social theory. The postmodernist holds that these traditional beliefs themselves lie at the root of what is wrong with the world today and therefore have no proper place in 21st-century thought and ethics. This last point is an important one because postmodern culture does not see itself as a rebellious teenager resisting authority it knows deep down to be legitimate. It firmly believes it has a duty to cast off the shackles of a primitive and corrupt Western psychology.

For the purposes of this book, it will be sufficient to describe postmodernism as that contemporary worldview that rejects the existence of absolute truth, fixed moral boundaries and traditional Western authority constructs. Four foundational assumptions of postmodernism that particularly come to bear on Christianity's present social context, summarized briefly below, are: pragmatism, pantheism, relativism, and egocentrism.

Pragmatism. Postmodern society embraces a two-level view of truth in how it views the physical world as compared with how it views non-material matters of ethics, morality and spirituality. In matters of the measurable, physical universe, little has changed. A statement is still viewed as 'true' if it is consistent with an objective fact of physical reality. For example, the statement, "The table is built out of maple" is 'true' if the table is, in physical fact, built out of maple.

However, outside of the scientific/physical realm, a 'true' statement need only pass the subjective test of being desirable, beneficial or practical for the one considering it. It need not correspond to any external reality or reference point. In questions of ethics, morality and spirituality, the test of truth is thoroughly results-oriented: "If it works for me, it's true." Within this framework, for example, the statement, "Jesus Christ is the Son of God" is 'true' for me if I believe this to be the case and if I have personally experienced some benefit from my belief. Postmodern thought sees no problem or contradiction in such a spiritual conviction being 'true' for one person and 'not true' for another person who finds no experiential reality in it.

Pantheism. This is the teaching that God is the universe and the universe is God. Pantheism is the emerging, dominant spirituality of Western culture today. The core belief of pantheism is that we are to worship the creation rather than the Creator. In its best light, it teaches that we must be good stewards of our environment. At its worst, pantheism teaches that humanity is simply a random biological phenomenon and has no distinctive status in the eyes of God whatsoever. The term "God," in fact, means something entirely different to someone born in 1983 than to someone born in 1943. The "god" of pantheism is no longer a volitional, personal being outside of creation who places moral obligations on his creatures. He, she or it is simply a life or energy "force," more reminiscent of *Star Wars* than of the Bible.

An adjunct principle of pantheism is the concept of collectivism, in which any distinctive significance of the individual is dissolved in the pre-eminence of the community. Pantheism speaks only of the future of a collective 'humanity:' the purpose of humanity, the destiny of humanity; as if all of humanity was one organism having a single mind, a single spirit and a single soul. The most dramatic worldview change from the 20th to the 21st centuries is the abandonment of monotheism, the belief in a personal God who exists outside of creation and knows each of his creatures individually. As society increasingly shifts away from the worship of the Creator toward the worship of creation, the significance of the individual is lost accordingly.

This transformation has led to a grave psychosocial crisis in our time because the deepest questions people ask no longer have satisfactory answers. "Does God know *me*?" "Does God love *me*?" "Does God have a purpose for *me*?" "Does God have a destiny for *me*? Correspondingly, high levels of despondency, depression and suicide increasingly afflict society; because we cannot maintain our psychological well being without knowing the answers to these questions.

Relativism. This is the belief that moral laws are adjustable as opposed to being absolute or universal. A generation ago, even secular society generally accepted the proposition that there was a fixed body of natural law governing human conduct and relationships; that human nature had to comply with certain unchanging obligations to self, family, community and government. Society recognized that natural law imposed its own punitive consequences for noncompliance and therefore, by common agreement, we submitted to this unavoidable cause-and-effect moral economy.

Postmodernism does not see itself as rebelling against natural law, but rather as denying its very existence! It views the concept of natural law as being cultural in origin rather than intrinsic to human nature. Today's relativism rejects the idea of an unchanging social anthropology. It believes that every generation (indeed, every individual!) is free to dismantle the framework of received wisdom and values and reinvent a new set of rules. It holds that *Homo sapiens* is a morally fluid and malleable species that can successfully adapt to whatever legal reference points it defines for itself in the present moment. Individual self-determination in morality is one of the highest values of postmodernism.

Egocentrism. I employ 'egocentrism' here in a very limited sense related to written communication. Until the mid-20th century, the meaning of the written word was generally held to reside in the writer's intention. The obligation of the reader/interpreter was to determine what the writer meant, respecting the writer's own social, political and cultural matrices. In this sense, the writer had a 'proprietary right' to his meaning that subsequent readers honored; his words continued to mean what he intended them to mean.

Egocentrism refers to that theory of meaning where a document means whatever the reader takes it to mean. The role of the writer is diminished, if not eliminated entirely. The text's meaning evolves based on the perspectives of each successive generation of readers. The cord connecting the writer to his words is severed and the reader assigns whatever meaning he determines to be acceptable within his own ideological context. "What it means to me today..." is now a common and respected prelude to discourse in our courts of law, our universities and even in our seminaries. Egocentrism is not just an accepted theory of interpretation in postmodern thought; it is the quintessential 21st-century protocol for invalidating the authority of established tradition and advancing one's own presuppositions.

* * *

These four assumptions are now thoroughly integrated into contemporary, postmodern society. They are not going back into the bottle. While the predominant reaction of Christians to this seismic ideological transformation of Western culture is generally negative, I will refrain from calling it so. The mini-series *Band of Brothers* contains a scene where, during the invasion of Normandy, a paratroop soldier reports in panic to his captain, "Sir, the enemy controls all sectors in every direction." The captain replies calmly, "Relax, son; we're paratroopers. We're supposed to be surrounded." Too often we lose sight of the fact that, "We're Christians; we're supposed to be surrounded by a pluralistic society." (In fact, we should be more alarmed if we're not than if we are!)

Christians' frustration with postmodernism too often arises out of their own agitation and inconvenience, not from a genuine hungering after God's honor. It is true that the social framework of forty years ago has crumbled and that the cost of this realignment has been high in terms of broken lives and social dysfunction. Yet, the "Christian" character of that society was a facade all along. There was much in the sagging superstructure of Western Christendom that needed to be dismantled. It had been complicit in too much racial, economic, gender and environmental injustice for too long and it could not have endured any longer.

Today's new social order offers Christianity the opportunity to define and understand itself more clearly and accurately than it has ever done before. I don't mean changing its doctrinal confession, but specifically: how Christianity understands its role and function in society. During the second half of the 20th century, foreign missions put itself through a complete methodological makeover. It successfully shed its former strategy of 'civilizing' foreign cultures; that is, indoctrinating them with a Western cultural veneer as a condition of becoming "Christian." It replaced this colonialist approach to ministry with one where every attempt is made to understand the worldview of the receptor culture and present a "de-Westernized" Jesus. As a result of this effort, foreign missionaries today are among the most culturally discerning workers in Christianity. Domestic Christianity has yet to achieve what foreign missions have already accomplished. It still needs to accept the reality that 21st-century postmodern society is as much a foreign culture as any ethnically distinct population requiring a missionary to adjust to a new language and unfamiliar thought systems. Western society looks like us, dresses like us and talks like us; but it is truly a different culture.

Christianity will need to abandon its traditional ways of interfacing with society because the well-worn paths into its institutions no longer have the 'welcome' signs up. It will also have to blow the dust off older strategies it neglected while it enjoyed its former favor in the public spotlight. Again, much of this redefinition will be for the better and will move Christianity closer to the biblical models of social interaction from which it strayed long ago.

It is some consolation that 21st-century Christianity no longer has access to the temptations of power that afflicted it in recent centuries. This shift is more of a blessing than we often realize. For in the new social order,

Christianity has lost not its best tools, but its least effective ones. The more political and social standing Christianity enjoys, the more of its energy it devotes to protecting and preserving that standing. The longer Christianity strives to hang onto its former influence, the more it will maintain an inward-looking maintenance mode. It is time for Christianity to awaken to the reality that it was this very position of weakness under the heel of the Roman Empire that provided the catalyst for its early growth. Perpetual comfort, stability and security are not consistent with fruitfulness. Christianity will not sustain its proper form and fruitfulness without this stress of opposition. Its dead branches require pruning. The winter cold must harden it to prepare for the coming spring. The summer heat needs to expose the seeds. The storm winds must scatter the seeds abroad.

The assumptions of pragmatism, pantheism, relativism and egocentrism are thoroughly woven into the fabric of postmodern society and they are not going away. Christianity needs to engage this present culture as it actually exists, not as we remember it. It is high time for 21st-century Christianity to conclude its season of mourning for a

20th-century world that is no more and get on with the work at hand. For when it does, it will soon find that the Holy Spirit has given it the right tools for the job and that it can abandon the ones it has dragged along from the last century.

2. The Battle of the Will

The Battle of the Will is Christianity's effort to impose the law on an unwilling society.

From the time of the Reformation onward, most Christian traditions have recognized God's administration of two distinct covenants, or governments in this present age: the government of creation, extending over all people; and the government of redemption, extending only over those who willingly submit to the lordship of Christ. Through his government of creation, God creates all people in his image, gives them wisdom and understanding through his Spirit, requires them to live justly with one another, hears their prayers, and honors their obedience to the laws of creation. The government of redemption is the Father's response to a broken creation in which he adopts into his family those who believe in his Son unto eternal life.

From Christianity's very beginning, working out just how these two governments inter-relate has been a pretty stormy business. During much of Christianity's development within its European context, the distinction between the two governments was blurred and, at times, nearly lost. The medieval crusades launched to recover the Holy Land for Christendom are universally recognized today as one of the great tragedies of Christian imperialism. How, we wonder, could these Christians have confused the spiritual goals of the kingdom of Christ with these cruel and bloody campaigns? Did they not understand that Christ sought to win people's hearts and devotion rather than conquer lands and walled cities? These misguided expeditions have left behind a residue of bitterness among the invaded peoples that continues to this day. Yet the crusades are only one example of Christianity's confusion over what, if any, authority it is to exercise within God's govern-ment of creation. For the most part, 21st-cen-tury Christianity appreciates the distinction between these two governments and the necessity of their separation. It would be hard to find many contemporary Christians who would advocate a reversion to the theocratic mindset of earlier European history where the authorities of Christianity and the state were merged into one.

We would be naïve, however, to conclude that this tension has been relieved altogether. Western Christianity no longer conducts crusades to wrestle countries away from the control of the "infidels"—at least not crusades using tactical military operations. Yet much of Christianity's effort today to exert its influence in society is driven by this same domineering, imperialistic spirit. We do not overtly seek to establish a Christian theocracy, but the temptation to press in that direction is very strong, especially since Christianity was the only game in town for such a long time. Just as the crusades sought to win back the Holy Land for Christ, Christians use a variety of strategies to win back our "Holy Land" from postmodernism. We recognize that the state should regard all religions as equal, but we also feel that Christianity is somehow "more equal." The oft-quoted premise is that ours is a Christian land founded on Christian principles and upheld by Christian values. This is allegedly our inheritance, our due and our right. We assert that our civil laws derive from Moses. We speak a language filled with biblical vocabulary and metaphor. We remember how recently our culture was molded around a theistic worldview and a linear view of history. So we nobly take up the fight against the "barbarians at the gate" who would strip away this Christian paradigm from our schools, our culture and our public institutions.

It would seem on the surface that every attempt to bring "the things of Christ" to bear on the public consciousness must in some way advance the gospel. Is it not preferable, we argue, that the name of Christ be heard wherever and however we are able make his name heard? The blunt answer to this question is 'No,' for Christ is only welcome in the government of creation by invitation. This is a hard lesson to digest, but the gospel message that we impose through exerting our legal rights is tainted and powerless. Joseph had no rightful place in the royal court of Egypt except at Pharaoh's decree that, "You shall be over my house and all my people shall be ruled according to your word." Zerubbabel became governor over occupied Jerusalem because the Lord stirred up the spirit of Cyrus, king of Persia to appoint him. Esther only kept her life in the presence of the king because he extended his golden sceptre toward her in favor. Daniel only served in Nebuchadnezzar's palace at the pleasure of the king, so that the Jews might learn the language and literature of the Chaldeans. Each of these citizens of the government of redemption had a radical influence for God, but none of them had any legal title to their places of influence.

21st-century Christianity needs to accept the reality that the government of creation has no obligation to recognize the government of redemption. The government of redemption is a government in exile: real and functioning; but, like the Son of Man, having no place to lay its head. From time to time, the government of creation will seek out a Joseph, a Zerubbabel, an Esther or a Daniel to provide various services that it holds to be in its own interest, but it may revoke this authorization at any time. Christians may complain, "But I am a citizen of the government of creation as well. I demand my equal rights, equal time and equal access." We need to clearly understand the impossibility this argument. The name of Christ brings an aroma to the government of creation unlike any other aroma. To those who love Jesus it brings life, hope, rest and peace. But for those who reject him, it accuses, it convicts, it judges and it exposes. Forcing the government of Christ upon the government of creation can only incite rebellion, friction and resentment. Jesus never chased after anyone who did not wish to follow him. He will not compel wandering sheep to follow him nor will he drive these sheep before him like cattle. Peter reminds Christians that their proper role in the world is as a community of aliens and temporary residents. No greater curse can befall Christianity than when it becomes the official religion of the land and gains a permanent seat in the halls of power.

Christianity's mandate is not to impose God's law upon the government of creation; it is to make disciples. And we can only make disciples of the willing. The fact that Western society submitted to this imposition for so long does not justify its continuance today. We should understand that the Great Commission commands us to "make disciples of all peoples," not to "disciple all nations." (The Greek *ethne* can be translated either "peoples" or "nations.") To the extent that we attempt to force a "Christian" legal grid upon a resistant society or nation, we set the cause of Christ back, not forward.

Our zeal to resist the 'de-Christianizing' of society too often arises out of our desire for continuity and stability. This is understandable, for change creates distress. Descent into lawlessness creates panic. For many Christians, it is a terrifying experience to see familiar values and traditions disintegrating into the moral chaos of our times. We can perhaps be comforted in realizing that God's intention for the government of creation is neither anarchy nor perfect stability. Anarchy impedes the work of the gospel, for the preaching of the gospel requires that God's messengers have access to orderly movement and commerce. God places his Josephs, his Zerubbabels, his Esthers and his Daniels in those strategic positions within the government of creation necessary to maintain the stability he deems necessary. Yet perfect stability is an anesthetic that deflates Christianity of its necessary urgency to advance Christ's kingdom. A comfortable Christianity is not a witnessing Christianity. Satisfied Christians do not move about and spread the gospel according to God's purposes.

It is not for us to know God's ultimate intent in directing the currents of the government of creation. The Lord puts hooks in the jaws of kings and leads them out according to his pleasure. In order to call a people of his own choosing, God raised up a new king over Egypt, who did not know Joseph and the deliverance Joseph had brought to Egypt. And so we see today a similar public departure from society's long-standing Christian under-girding. As painful as it can be for Christianity to watch this exodus, it is critically important that we do not block the exit. Moses declares, "I call heaven and earth as witnesses today against you, that I have set before you life and death, blessing and cursing; therefore choose life, that both you and your descendants may live." Christianity is to freely allow each one to choose the things of God (or not) according to this pattern.

Living as we do in a progressive, liberal democracy, it is difficult for us to appreciate the radical nature of God's invitation in its context. At this formative stage in the history of civilization, the idea of a sovereign ruler calling his subjects to choose to submit to him is unheard of. The kings of the ancient Near East ruled by violence and absolute force. The concept of self-determination had not yet begun to surface in social or political theory. And yet Yahweh extended this open invitation for Israel to choose to submit to him or not, as each person saw fit.

And so we find here in the Mosaic Law, that most revolutionary seed of Jeffersonian thought, of governments "deriving their just powers from the consent of the governed;" a concept that would not find its full application in human affairs until the early democracies of post-Reformation Europe. I wonder how often we think of God in this light: that he continually asks us to choose life, but never forces life upon us. Where else can we find such an offer? Our mothers force us to eat our peas. Our teachers make us do our homework. Our fathers kick us out of the nest to find a job. The government makes us pay our taxes. But the invitation of God is always to choose. The gospels record that the multitudes followed Jesus for a while, but the time came when many of his disciples went back and walked with Him no more. Do we find him arguing with those who chose to leave, pressing and coercing them to get back into line? We do not, for this is neither God's purpose nor his nature.

Our capacity to choose is one of the cornerstones of biblical anthropology: that God created humanity in his own image; and a central element of that image is free choice, or the capacity to make ethical and moral choices.

And having given us the capacity, God respects that boundary and does not trespass, even to our own hurt and sorrow. God placed the man and the woman in the Garden where they had the opportunity to choose. They chose poorly and suffered death, even as God knew they would; yet he did not intervene. And even now, he watches over each of us and sees our various follies, our stubbornness and our stupidity. He will offer warning and counsel, but he does not resist us. He sets before us life and death, blessing and cursing; but if we insist on death and cursing, God does not revoke his gift, saying, "Enough is enough! This free choice business has gone too far." He only calls us to consider and choose life.

It is necessary that God respect the boundary he himself set in allowing us to choose. This is the essence of human free agency. If God prevented us from choosing death, he would, by reciprocity, also prevent us from choosing life. For if we do not have a real capacity to choose death, then the ability to choose life is an illusion. I once worked in an office where the manager made a great show of releasing staff to make their own decisions and work independently. But, in fact, every project he delegated had a string tied to it. If you didn't do it the way he would have done it, he pulled it back and took it over himself. He was a micro-manager. God is not like that. When he calls us to choose, he means it and he will not revoke that choice.

Even in humanity's fallen condition, God has not revoked our capacity to choose. Moses' invitation to Israel and the promise of life in Jesus Christ rests on the proposition that we have a real capacity to choose life; that whoever we are, whatever we have done, however we may have failed and fallen in the past, we retain the capacity to choose life over death.

God's call always appeals to this capacity to choose. There is something about a call to choose that resonates with the human soul. People will not willingly respond to threat or force, but the human heart rejoices to follow by choice what is right and true. Christianity's greatest achievements are realized when it calls people to freely decide whether they will choose God or not. It is amazing the energy, the effort and the sacrifice that people will apply to that which they have freely chosen.

On the other hand, where Christianity has used coercion and manipulation its results have been very limited. For the first 300 years of its existence Christianity was composed primarily of those who had chosen to participate of their own volition. Then in A.D. 313, Emperor Constantine did something that was to determine the course and character of Western Christianity for the next 1,500 years. The Edict of Milan made Christianity legal for the first time. From there, it was only a hop, skip and a jump to making Christianity mandatory and all other religions illegal. The history of European civilization is essentially the story of universal Christianity, forced on everyone whether they were willing or not. Under the auspices of the gospel, we see the European nations subjugated and controlled, we see non-European cultures exploited and enslaved, and millions of people in both settings forced to endure compulsive conversion and baptism.

Such coercion was not the Father's heart and it was certainly not consistent with God's own commitment to honoring the choice of human will. God is more like a Costco host than a security guard. You know: those folks in white aprons who serve up food samples at the back of the store. How intimidating is a Costco host? You wander by and they ask you if you would like to try a bite of some tasty snack. Not a huge portion; just enough to see if you like it. But if you don't want to try it, it's your choice. And then, if you like it enough, maybe you'll buy the product. But if you don't, it's your choice. They understand that very few tasters will become buyers, but a few will. The psalmist likewise pleads invitingly, "Oh, taste and see that the Lord is good."

How did Christianity stray so far from this model? Why is it that Christianity has more often behaved like an overweight security guard who strong-arms you in the aisle and forces you to buy a case of stewed tomatoes you don't really want? There's nothing wrong with the tomatoes. They may be very fine tomatoes. But we don't appreciate that which is forced upon us, do we? It is the course of this world to impose one's will upon the unwilling. Armies march to war so that the victors can impose their will upon the vanquished. Political parties work to win elections so that they can impose their will upon the minority. Even Christianity, when it finds itself in a position of political advantage, cannot resist the temptation to inflict its will upon the unwilling. What a refreshing contrast we find in Jesus, who declares: "...let him who thirsts come. Whoever desires, let him take the water of life freely." This is the character of the God who calls us to choose.

Free agency is a critical element of human identity because our dignity is wrapped up in this capacity. The greatest recognition we can give to a person's dignity is to honour his capacity to choose. A person who has lost nearly everything else will cling ever more tightly to his free agency. For that dignity may be all he has left. One of the great errors we make in ministering to human need is to make someone else's choice for them. For in doing this, we strip them of their dignity. And then we are surprised when, in the long run, their problems go unresolved.

Oprah once did a show on supervised teenage drinking parties. This is where parents bring their children together in one house on grad night, give them enough booze to drink themselves stupid, and then force them to sleep it off before they're allowed to leave the house. The rationale is that, "Our kids are going to drink anyway, so let's facilitate it in a safe setting. At least they won't kill themselves on the highway." The underlying belief of these parents is that their children cannot choose life. If left to themselves they will surely choose death, so that choice must be denied them.

The more I thought about this, I said, "OK, maybe these parents prevented a car crash; but they stole something from their children that was very precious. They stole their free agency and, as a result, their dignity." They said to their children, "You are brute beasts. You have no capacity to choose life, so we will revoke your choice and give you this instead." They may not have given their children death, but they certainly did not give them life.

Contrast what these parents did to one of the first decisions the apostles had to make. Christianity was brand new and it faced an issue that was very strange to these leaders, all of whom were Jews. Jewish society had produced a very disciplined culture where everyone was under the law. They were raised on the Law of Moses and knew what conduct was required. But when Christianity started to fill up with Gentiles, it faced a dilemma. The Gentiles came from every kind of diverse, polytheistic background. They did not have the law. Their consciences had not been well trained to know right from wrong. What would Christianity require of these Gentiles? Maybe the grace of the gospel meant that they should be left alone to live in whatever way they saw fit.

So the apostles met and prayed over this question. And the answer they came up with offers an enduring wisdom: "For it seemed good to the Holy Spirit, and to us, to lay upon you no greater burden than these necessary things: that you abstain from things offered to idols, from blood, from things strangled, and from sexual immorality. If you keep yourselves from these, you will do well." The Gentiles were not required to keep the whole Law of Moses, but they were required to submit to a basic morality that was necessary for their proper spiritual development. In short, if they wanted to choose life, this was the decision set before them.

These leaders could have committed either of two errors here, both of which would have been equally disastrous. First, they could have heaped upon these new converts the full weight of centuries of rabbinical laws and Jewish traditions. But in the liberty of the Christian gospel, this was neither necessary nor appropriate. Second, they could have allowed the Gentiles into the church and required nothing of them. But this would have denied the Gentiles the opportunity to exercise their God-given free agency and choose for themselves the life God offered to them. And so we find in this decision the proper choice in the proper measure.

We don't know how many of the Gentile Christians accepted these conditions. I'm sure that some of them left when the leaders called them to choose. There are always people who are curious about Jesus, but they find other things more attractive in the present. And when God calls them to choose between the two, they're gone. A person who is given the opportunity to choose life will surprise us. We look at people and we think we know what they are made of, how they will respond and what capacity they have to choose. But we read in Proverbs that "Counsel in the heart of man is like deep water." We do not know the secrets of each one's heart and how he will respond to God's invitation.

We can never suppose that people are too fragile to be called to choose. Those who choose life and those who choose death will surprise us. God calls us to choose life because he has created us to choose and it is only in our choosing that we find our true identity as creatures made in his image. Christianity can no longer afford the abuses of authority it exercised in the past. It needs to accept the role of God's Costco hosts in the 21st century. Christianity must allow a postmodern society the freedom to choose Jesus—and then bless it even when it doesn't.

3. The Battle of the Flesh

The Battle of the Flesh is Christianity's resistance to lawlessness for the sake of its own comfort and stability.

...there is a lion outside! I shall be slain in the streets!

Proverbs

There is that brand of religion that wrings its hands in detached disgust over the deterioration of our social fabric in the 21st century. It complains not because God's heart is broken, not because his sheep are scattered across the landscape, but because its own comfortable equilibrium has been upset by change and lawlessness. This superficial spirituality fails to perceive that change is the resistance that builds the muscles of faith; that when it faces no change it grows self-sufficient and self-indulgent.

The body of Christ can only transform or die, for that which is alive can never simply sustain. The undoing of the rich fool who built bigger barns was that he tried to insulate himself from change. And in that, his attitude was inconsistent with life. Therefore the Lord required his soul from him that night. The history of Christianity is that of the Holy Spirit compelling change and tradition resisting it. Therefore, the Spirit has always worked his change through the small, the weak and the obscure; because the powerful and the learned would not have it. Even faith cannot remain fixed, but must face new problems that demand new perspectives and adjustments. Change gives life its definition, for without change or its promise we could have no sense of fear, hope, expectation, apprehension, surprise, sorrow or joy; no appreciation of any transition from the present to the future. We would float aimlessly in a state between sleep and wakefulness, having no need to wonder what lies around the next corner.

The stability our souls pursue is unequally yoked with the regime of change our spirits require, and this speaks to the complexity of human nature. We expend so much of our energy building buffers against change, yet the Lord constantly thrusts change upon us. Stable Christians don't move because their inertia is greater than their dreams. They don't risk because they have nothing to gain. They don't explore because they are content where they are. They don't question because they need no answers. They don't pray because they are satisfied with what they have. They have little faith because all they expect is already before their eyes. One of the most brutally honest sermons I ever heard was one in which a pastor told his congregation that several of them shouldn't be there any more; that God had long ago nudged them on and they had resisted him.

The biblical view of change is a difficult meal to digest, for it contains many strange ingredients unpalatable to popular religious sentiment. An appropriate starting point is God's prophetic proclamation to Pharaoh, "But indeed for this purpose I have raised you up, that I may show my power in you, and that my name may be declared in all the earth." When Moses spoke these words to Pharaoh, six of the plagues upon Egypt had already passed. Pharaoh's view of reality was changing. He was learning that he did not control things the way he thought he did. The

Lord essentially said to him, "Pharaoh, I've got an agenda you don't even know about. The only reason you're here is that you fill a role in what I want to accomplish."

The primary lesson we learn from this passage is that God controls history. The language of "raising up" is the term that God applies to himself to describe his supervision of world affairs. God is always saying, "I will raise up this king or that nation to accomplish what I want done." Sometimes God's action is directed toward the righteous. God raised up good King Asa who was the instrument of the Lord's will. In Luke's gospel we find the "raised up" formula referring to the Messiah, himself. We generally find it a morally acceptable theology that God raises up obedient servants to do his bidding.

But this picture takes on an entirely different flavor when we realize that the Bible uses this same language about the unrighteous. "I have raised you up, Pharaoh. I have caused you to prosper as the king of an oppressive, idolatrous superpower. Everything you see around you I have prepared because I have a purpose that is higher than human wisdom." We see that Pharaoh is a ruthless dictator. He does whatever he has to do to ensure the survival of his empire. The children of Israel suffered grievously under Pharaoh. And then God reveals that he, himself, raised up this tyrant who works such monstrous evil. The prophet Habakkuk was astounded when he learned that God acts this way; that he is "raising up the Chaldeans, a bitter and hasty nation which marches through the breadth of the earth, to possess dwelling places that are not theirs." The Chaldeans will meet with their judgment later on, but for the time being God sustains them because he has a purpose that this merciless army will serve.

The Bible clearly teaches that God raises up both good and evil agents to accomplish his purposes. He does not create evil, but he directs it toward his ultimate purposes and does not judge it immediately. God is managing history and bringing its affairs to his chosen conclusion. I want to contrast this view of history with another viewpoint that circulates widely among Christians today.

It is often held that Satan is in charge of this world; that he directs the nations and he raises up his own leaders to manage world affairs. Yet God cast Satan to the earth; he did not grant the devil authority over it. Satan is nothing more than a condemned criminal awaiting the execution of the judge's sentence. Satan is only the god of this age in the sense that he influences people through deception, temptation and manipulation. It is in this sense that Jesus calls Satan the ruler of this world. Satan is exactly like the leader of a street gang that controls an area of a city as its "turf." He holds no title, legal rights or delegated authority pertaining to his turf. He is simply an outlaw.

Satan's claim to ownership of the world's kingdoms was his own assertion and was a lie. God grants Satan limited freedom to roam the earth because it suits God's purposes. Satan can only afflict individuals directly with God's permission. Satan is not omnipresent, but is a spatially limited being. Satan's attacks on Job, Peter and Paul are shown to be specific allowances from God. At all other times, Satan is limited to impeding Christians' work through indirect temptation and deception.

Through misunderstanding the status of Satan in this age, people have attributed to him authority that belongs only to the Lord. God runs the world and Satan does not. The reason we have a difficult time believing that God is in control of the evils and tragedies of history is that our priorities are not God's priorities. We strive to maintain stability. We desire peaceful relations between nations rather than conflict. We desire a stable economy so that business can run smoothly and prosper. We desire environmental stability, as opposed to flood, drought, famine and disease. And we naturally assume that God desires these things in all times and places too.

But God is a shaker. Whereas we constantly try to stabilize our environment, God comes along and shakes it up: "'I will shake all nations, and the desired of all nations will come, and I will fill this house with glory,' says the Lord Almighty." God maintains a measured level of instability in the world. Jesus had to set his disciples straight on this point: Do you think that I came to bring peace on earth? No way! I did not come to bring peace but a sword. God raises up some leaders and nations which are relatively righteous. He raises up other powers which are deceived by Satan and work evil.

The Bible offers two reasons for God supporting Pharaoh and his oppressive government. First: "That I may show my power in you." Through Pharaoh's experiences, the whole world would learn of God's power.

Our default perspective of the universe is that humanity is the headline player and that God is answerable to us for any jostling about that we find inconvenient. But God raises up Pharaoh and directs all of history for his own purposes and glory. It is only with considerable discipline that we are able to bend our thinking back to the reality that God's affairs are all about him—not about us.

Second: "That my name may be declared in all the earth." In order for God's name to be declared in all the earth, he needs his messengers to move about and carry it to all the earth. When life is stable and secure, people don't move. The migration of peoples to other lands is almost always the result of environmental stresses, political oppression or economic instability. When we understand the Great Commission as being Christianity's #1 priority, we would naturally expect that God would facilitate the movement of people to other lands. In fact, that is exactly what God does. When God raises up kings and leaders, he doesn't necessarily choose the ones who would produce the most peaceful and stable world. But in his own sovereign will, he chooses a line-up that will maintain a controlled balance of stability and instability.

Now these are difficult teachings to live with, aren't they? It's much easier to believe that in every place and at all times God desires peace and stability to prevail (the error of liberal theology). However, the Bible doesn't teach that. This theology of instability has far-reaching implications for the Christian who takes it to heart. For one thing, it cautions Christians against becoming too nationalistic (the error of conservative theology). A Christian is to work for the betterment of his country, he is to respect his government and be a productive citizen. But a Christian also realizes that God reserves the right to cause nations to rise and fall according to his sovereign will. When Jeremiah prophesied that Jerusalem would fall to the Babylonians, he stood alone. All of the other prophets had been corrupted by their political alliances and blinded by their nationalism. They could not accept what God was going to do.

The Christian who understands this theology also avoids getting involved in any utopian programs for the perfection of this world. He understands that the evils that afflict humanity are not going to disappear until the final Day. The wheat and the tares will indeed grow together until the end. So the Christian lives in a very curious relationship to society. He is to defend the cause of the oppressed, yet he knows that injustice will continue. He feeds the hungry, yet he knows that the hungry will always be with us. The Christian is to be a peacemaker and a reconciler, and yet he knows that God will use wars for his sovereign purposes. The Christian is to prophetically call for righteousness in government, yet he knows that God raises up the unrighteous in order that his power may be shown through them.

When the apostle John wrote to us, "Do not love the world," he meant much more than the avoidance of sensual luxuries and pleasures. But he warned us that Christians are to live with a sober understanding of God's purposes in shaking the world. It is the ultimate irony that 21st-century society most readily associates Christianity with stability, the status quo and conservative ideology; for the Christian's original role in the Roman world was that of iconoclast and revolutionary. We are not to become so attached to our culture, our country or the comforts of stability that we lose sight of the God who removes kings and shakes nations.

Christians are to be a going people. They are to be about God's work as they circulate through his world as aliens and strangers in a foreign land. Somewhat predictably, the Christians who complain the loudest about postmodern culture are the ones who are standing still. It is their immobility that makes them feel like grasshoppers among giants in this age of social upheaval. But when we respond to Christ's call and take up the daily work he gives us to do, the daunting horizons of change will retreat to their proper place in our spiritual landscape. To the degree that Christians can attain to this perspective, nearly all of their anxiety over the postmodern lawlessness of 21st-century society will dissipate into the balm of God's sovereign rule over his creation.

4. The Battle of the Soul

The Battle of the Soul is Christianity's unrealistic demand that those without the Spirit of God keep his law.

> *...the natural man does not receive the things of the Spirit of God, for they are foolishness to him; nor can he know them, because they are spiritually discerned.*
>
> *1 Corinthians*

The Bible defines the natural man—literally, "the man of animal soul,"—by that which he lacks: the indwelling Spirit of God. He is distinguished from the animals in that he bears the image of God and has a conscience that discerns right from wrong. But he is identified with the animals in that he only has the capacity to comprehend the values and aspirations of this present, visible world. The natural man has not weighed the things of the Spirit and rejected them; but he **cannot** weigh them or even recognize them. He may aspire to a high moral code, exemplary ethical conduct and sacrificial service to others, but his motivation is wholly sensual, centered on the tangible satisfactions offered by the world he can see, touch and measure.

It was not so very long ago in Christianity's history that such outward evidence identified one as a "Christian." If a natural man presented himself "as a Christian should," that was proof enough. Christianity even divided the world geographically into Christendom and the "heathen" nations, convinced that the "civilizing" of non-Western "pagan" cultures was an essential prerequisite to evangelism. The pioneer missionary efforts of the 17th and 18th centuries were harshly criticized at the time for holding the naïve view that the so-called "savage, uncivilized mind" even had the capacity to respond to the gospel. We regard this attitude as racist colonialism today—and rightly so. Yet our hindsight does not change the reality that it was a view honestly held in its time, and many selfless missionaries sacrificed their lives to bring civilization to other cultures in the name of Christ. Contemporary Christianity no longer holds to this elitist distortion of the gospel, however, there remains a residue of this error in our thinking: that the natural man who lives in a "Christian" culture somehow has a spiritual "leg up" on one who does not.

But there are only two categories of spiritual condition: the Spirit-filled man and the natural man; not a gradual, evolutionary advancement from darkness to light as we often suppose. The law is acceptable only to the renewed mind, can be taught only to the renewed mind and will only be comprehended by the renewed mind. This limitation was not so obvious in recent centuries when the two cultures of Christianity and Western society were so finely intertwined. Christianity regarded the whole of Western civilization as its congregation. Of course, this perspective was never a reality in fact. The difference today is that the momentous fracture between Christianity and postmodern society has brought to light that which was always true: those who are not born of the Spirit do not receive or understand the things of the Spirit. The Christian, having the Spirit of God, can rejoice with the psalmist: "Oh, how I love your law!" The natural man without the Spirit can never attain to this perspective. He can only regard the law as an accuser and a constraint on his freedom.

Perhaps the greatest contradiction in Christianity's interaction with society is its theological confession, on the one hand, that only Christians have spiritual understanding of the law; and its insistence, on the other, that society conform to the demands of the law. Christianity agrees with the apostle (at least in theory) that there is a blindness upon the natural man regarding the things of God that is spiritual rather than cognitive in its essence. It admits that teaching, argument, logical persuasion, empirical evidence, statistics or rational dialogue cannot cure this blindness. Yet Christians continue to expect that our schools, our governments, our courts, our military and every other secular institution should accept the law as their fundamental reference point, requiring of the natural man that which he can never offer. 21st-century Christianity simply does not take its own biblical anthropology seriously and consistently! It expects those whose minds are not renewed to somehow function at a spiritual level accessible only to those who have received the Spirit. This misconception seeps almost unnoticed into a number of institutions in Christian culture.

One example of this is the explosive growth of virtual Christianity. The practice of broadcasting the celebration and exposition of the law assumes that the natural man can enter into some limited level of Christian discipleship. We should subject virtual Christianity to greater scrutiny, for the broadcasting of Christian worship services and teaching is commonplace today. Certainly Christianity should use every medium available to spread the gospel—electronic and otherwise. But the indiscriminate broadcasting of the law is another matter altogether. Christian ministries who use this kind of broadcasting would not contemplate that any balancing of advantages against disadvantages is even necessary.

Christianity needs to carefully manage the distribution of its "pearls" in accordance with the reality of human nature. When Christianity mixes gospel and law, the natural man only hears the law. There is clearly a danger in proclaiming the law to those who can only regard it as an unreasonable burden. It is possible to make the things of God too accessible to those who cannot spiritually discern them. The Bible always requires some effort from the inquirer to divert from his own affairs to look into spiritual matters—"I will now turn aside and see this great sight, why the bush does not burn." Virtual Christianity disregards this principle. It is not to Christianity's credit that it goes to such extreme efforts to spoon feed its treasures to someone who would not drive ten minutes to explore them for himself. So the proverb laments, "A lazy man buries his hand in the bowl, and will not so much as bring it to his mouth again."

Virtual Christianity sends the message that Christian spirituality is essentially a non-responsive and cognitive endeavour. Christianity certainly has a cognitive element, but it requires our full physical, emotional and relational participation as well. We are to worship together, pray for one another, encourage and admonish one another, and share in each other's joys and sorrows. The virtual Christians who appear on television, on the other hand, are better looking, have slicker testimonies, sing more inspiring music, preach better sermons and have greater faith than the "real" people the viewer has to deal with where he actually lives. He doesn't have to actually get to know virtual Christians, so they are always spiritual, scrubbed clean, smiling and filled with the presence of God. Their Christianity is always exciting and victorious. God is always doing something marvellous in their virtual lives. This electronic world gradually becomes the viewer's reality and he grows increasingly frustrated with the imperfect, ordinary spirituality he sees in his real world.

But the Lord calls his shepherds to present their whole lives to their disciples on an ongoing basis. Their conduct, character, and spiritual fruit are to be the validation of their message. They are to carefully discern when and how to dispense the law. Virtual Christianity eliminates this crucial aspect of ministry entirely. The home viewer has many teachers, but few fathers. Genuine Christian life is not a two-dimensional commercial that can be broadcast to someone who has made no greater effort to respond than to press a button on his remote control. It is a delusion to suppose that the experience of Christians gathered together can be broadcast indiscriminately and retain any of the reality of the Spirit's presence. At best, this is a caricature of true spiritual life. At the worst, it subjects God's law to ridicule and cheapening by mockers—"Do not speak in the hearing of a fool, for he will despise the wisdom of your words."

Christianity's confusion about the spiritual capability of the natural man is also evident in its approach to evangelism. The natural man, even if he has lived his entire life with a church on every other corner, does not receive the things of the Spirit of God. The natural man has only one spiritual transaction available to him and required of him: to believe in Jesus Christ according to the gift of faith God provides to him. Until this regenerating process is accomplished, his mind is incapable of grasping the array of legal transactions we set before him. It is truly remarkable to consider the number of Christian discipleship regimes we illegitimately include in the task of evangelism, hardly recognizing the impossibility of our expectations.

Christianity too often requires those who would believe in Christ to act as if they already have. Much of Christianity's evangelism involves forms of "pre-discipleship," an attempt to initiate certain processes of spiritual life in people prior to a profession of faith. A close examination of this practice is illuminating because it reveals the extent to which 21st-century Christianity attempts to disciple the natural man, improperly confusing the distinctly separate functions of gospel and law. A brief summary of six steps commonly included in "How to Become a Christian" materials will illustrate this practice. At best, these requirements accomplish nothing. At worst, they do significant harm.

1. Recognize you have sinned. This is the most common starting point for our presentation of the gospel, yet its basis is cultural rather than biblical. The natural man is spiritually blind and really can't recognize much at all about his own sinfulness. Indeed, Paul states, "I would not have known sin except through the law." At best, the natural man may view certain specific acts condemned by society such as murder, theft or lying to be sin, but his mind is in a state of futility and his understanding is darkened. He is unable to comprehend sin as being the essence of his nature, and God does not require him do so. God only requires that a person believe in Jesus Christ, not that he comprehend his own condemnation under the law. He may not be aware of any legal culpability at the moment he believes.

The essence of the gospel is that God sent his son into the world to die and then raised him from the dead, that whoever believes in his name should have everlasting life. God makes no such demand on people to correctly assess their own sin as a prerequisite to receiving eternal life. The Ethiopian eunuch asked of Phillip, "'What hinders me from being baptized?' Then Philip said, 'If you believe with all your heart, you may.' And he answered and said, 'I believe that Jesus Christ is the Son of God.'" Christianity's mandate is to proclaim this gospel to the world and preach the law to believers. Instead, we all too often do just the opposite!

2. Confess your sin to Jesus. The Bible nowhere requires the confession of sin as a condition of gaining eternal life, yet we inevitably place this legal obligation on those who would believe in Christ. The account of the bronze serpent illustrates how this is inappropriate:

And the people spoke against God and against Moses: "Why have you brought us up out of Egypt to die in the wilderness? For there is no food and no water, and our soul loathes this worthless bread." So the Lord sent fiery serpents among the people, and they bit the people; and many of the people of Israel died. Therefore the people came to Moses, and said, "We have sinned, for we have spoken against the Lord and against you; pray to the Lord that He take away the serpents from us." So Moses prayed for the people. Then the Lord said to Moses, "Make a fiery serpent, and set it on a pole; and it shall be that everyone who is bitten, when he looks at it, shall live." So Moses made a bronze serpent, and put it on a pole; and so it was, if a serpent had bitten anyone, when he looked at the bronze serpent, he lived.

Although the Israelites (or at least some of them) confessed their sin, the Lord did not associate this confession with the remedy for death. He did not say, "The one who is bitten shall live when he looks at the fiery serpent, ***but only if he confesses his sin!***" The only requirement to live was to look at the serpent and the only requirement to gain eternal life is to believe in Jesus.

Confession of sin is a privilege of the Christian, allowing him to return to a position of blessing and fellowship with God after he has wandered away. John states, "If we confess our sins, he is faithful and just to forgive us our sins, and to cleanse us from all unrighteousness." This is a promise to the Christian, not to the unbeliever.

3. Ask for forgiveness. We commonly include this instruction as part of the "sinner's prayer," but forgiveness of sins is a **consequence** of believing in Jesus, not a **condition** of receiving eternal life. Forgiveness is the execution of a legal obligation. It is that removal of an outstanding debt or obligation made possible by the payment of the debt or the fulfillment of the obligation. If someone could receive forgiveness of sins before believing in Jesus, then there would be no reason to believe in him and he went to the cross unnecessarily!

Before a person becomes a Christian, he has no access to forgiveness of sins, so why would we instruct him to ask for forgiveness as a condition of receiving eternal life? The apostle teaches, "He has delivered us from the power of darkness and conveyed us into the kingdom of the Son of His love, in whom we have redemption through His blood, the forgiveness of sins." We only **have** forgiveness of sins **after** we are in Christ.

4. Ask him to help you turn away from your old life, and commit to doing so. This is the doctrine of repentance. Repentance means to have a change of mind and turn around. The natural man may regret the consequences of sin in his life. He may even wish to forsake his sin and turn away from his old life. But he cannot do so because repentance is a spiritual transaction that is inaccessible to the natural man. "...the carnal mind is enmity against God; for it is not subject to the law of God, nor indeed can be. So then, those who are in the flesh cannot please God."

Repentance is a gift of God that flows out of the new life in Christ. It is not an act of human will that can precede belief. "Him God has exalted to His right hand to be Prince and Savior, to **give** repentance to Israel and forgiveness of sins." And again: "When they heard these things they became silent; and they glorified God, saying, 'Then God has also **granted** to the Gentiles repentance to life.'"

5. Ask the Lord into your life, to be in control and guide you. Inviting the Lord "into your life" does not result in eternal life. This relatively recent concept of "inviting" or "accepting"

Jesus into my life really runs contrary to God's intention with those he calls. God's purpose with us is literally to kill us; to destroy our lives; to undo our lives; to bury our lives; and then to raise up a new life that he can direct to his own glory. So when we speak of inviting Jesus into my life, this suggests that the Lord is on my turf, under my conditions for the purpose of achieving my priorities. And for many people, that's exactly the case. They have a "Jesus" whom they have fashioned according to their own desires and they keep him around only as long as he fits in with all the other "my life" stuff they hang onto. This is exactly what happened when a Pharisee invited the Lord "into his life" and had him home for supper. But he got upset when Jesus forgave the sins of a prostitute and after that, Jesus wasn't welcome in the Pharisee's life anymore.

A person only becomes a Christian through his act of belief. Belief is a volitional act of the heart: "For with the heart one believes unto righteousness, and with the mouth confession is made unto salvation." So we are not to confuse inviting the Lord to "come into your life" with believing in the name of Jesus unto eternal life.

6. Determine to follow him, through the direction of His Spirit and the study of his Word. The natural man has no concept of the challenges and trials encountered in following Jesus. He only has one unopposed, completely-in-control, fallen nature. He knows nothing of the conflict between the flesh and the Spirit. It is deceptive to encourage the natural man to make a commitment to follow Jesus when he does not have the capacity to understand what this means and when he does not have the Holy Spirit to enable him to do so.

* * *

Christianity's expectation that people incorporate all these steps into a confession of faith in Jesus reveals a serious misunderstanding of the limitations of the futile and darkened mind of the natural man who has not yet believed. It is worse than just theologically inaccurate. It leads new Christians to suppose that they had more to do with gaining eternal life than they did. They can fail to understand that the gift of eternal life was all of God and none of their own effort. As a result, these Christians can begin their spiritual lives with a deficient understanding of grace.

A sign of a healthy Christian is that he is always concerned about the *quality* of his discipleship and never concerned about the *status* of his sonship. He lives in the reality that: "...you did not receive a spirit that makes you a slave again to fear, but you received the Spirit of sonship." Imposing these conditions on people prior to faith can make them think that the status of their adoption depends on their faithfulness. If they had to go through six steps of commitment to become children of God, then they sometimes feel that that their eternal life is degraded or even in doubt when they stumble in these six areas later on. "Have I maintained all those six conditions of obtaining eternal life that they brought me through? Does my heavenly Father really love me? Am I good enough? Am I really a member of God's family or am I just a hired servant who is only welcome in his house as long as my performance measures up?"

I can hardly overemphasize the problems and difficulties Christianity causes for itself (and for society) through waging the battle of the soul. The natural man who does not have the Spirit will either distort the mysteries of God or be crushed under the weight of the law. Wise stewards of these mysteries will consider carefully when and where they distribute them. For this reason, we need to always keep this single condition of receiving eternal life in view. God simply calls the natural man to believe that Christ is the Son of God—nothing more and nothing less. God places only one condition on those who would receive everlasting life: that they believe in the name of Jesus Christ. The act of believing is the only possible condition of receiving eternal life because belief is only possible after God grants the gift of faith to those whom he calls: "For by grace you have been saved through faith, and that not of yourselves; it is the gift of God." This one word 'believe' represents all the natural man must do and all he can do to gain eternal life.

5. The Battle of the Mind

The Battle of the Mind is Christianity's efforts to answer postmodernism's rational objections to the law .

Do not answer a fool according to his folly, lest you also be like him.

Proverbs

Apologetics is that discipline of the theological task that seeks to explain the basis of one's Christian faith. It derives its justification largely from Peter's admonition that the Christian is to, "always be ready to give a defence to everyone who asks you a reason for the hope that is in you." Several streams of apologetics have emerged over the centuries. Some give priority to the inward and subjective witness of the Holy Spirit's work in each one's heart. Others stress that Christian belief is consistent with natural theology and the rational assessment of empirical data. Still others emphasize God's objective revelation in his Son and in the Bible.

It is not my intent to wade too deeply into the pool of Christian apologetics and argue the merits of one view over another. I wish instead to highlight two primary motives for any Christian apologetic: (1) to answer questions about the faith from genuine seekers of Jesus and (2) to satisfy government authorities that the kingdom of Christ is not a threat to the state. However, Peter's admonition does not direct Christians to engage critics who object to the faith on a purely rational level. The apostles repeatedly caution against disputes on those terms. By their very nature, these interactions can never lead to faith in Christ. Christianity's efforts to answer rational criticism serve largely to preserve and enhance our own reputations. But apologetics is the defence of one's hope in Christ, not a defence of the reputation of the one who hopes.

We need to focus on this subtle, but crucial distinction. A great deal of our effort in explaining, defending and justifying our Christian beliefs to postmodern culture is not so much advocating for Christ as it is the vanity of advocating for our own intellectual and social reputations. We want to make the case that we are rational and respectable in our convictions about Jesus Christ. We want to be recognized as logical, clear-thinking intellectuals. We want to compete on all the same academic levels as the world and to be found worthy in its sight. Christianity has very little appetite today to accept the shame of the cross and to be accounted fools by the world. We have become ashamed of the blatant simplicity and uncompromising barbarity of the cross. We cannot tolerate the world's ridicule. When the world distorts and misrepresents our convictions we are outraged. This visceral reaction indicates that our advocacy for the legitimacy of our Christian faith is really all about justifying ourselves, not about proclaiming Jesus. Above all else, we do not want to be seen as fools. Yet that is precisely whom God calls us to be, for God calls us to proclaim a hidden wisdom that cannot be seen or vindicated at the bench of human reason.

One of postmodern thought's favorite stratagems to dismiss Christianity is the assertion that "primitive" civilization invented God solely to fill in the gaps in its scientific knowledge. It asserts that humanity's growing understanding of the physical world has now ushered God off to the retirement home accordingly. My concern is not with postmodernism's shallow contrivance, but rather with Christianity's all too willing readiness to play at this game. For when it submits its confession to the scrutiny of empirical examination, Christianity accepts by default postmodernism's assertion that such an assessment by the rational mind is a legitimate enterprise.

But Christianity's efforts to justify faith to the rational mind use tools that were never intended to perform that task. Christian faith is not irrational, but it is definitely suprarational; it is a transaction that occurs outside the sphere of rationality. As creatures made in the image of God, human beings are complex creatures. We have a spirit through which we perceive matters in the heavenly realm, physical senses that measure the material world and certain faculties—the mind and the heart—that crossover and relate to both. Simply put, we are to limit our use of these faculties to their intended applications. If we attempt to discern spiritual reality using rational faculties designed to measure the visible world, we will get unreliable results.

When the word of God comes to us, we have certain faculties that receive that word and others that process and respond to it. The anthropology of belief is laid out accordingly: "And how shall they believe in Him of whom they have not heard?... For with the heart one believes unto righteousness, and with the mouth confession is made unto salvation." Our ears receive the message of Christ, the heart is the faculty of belief, and then we confess our faith with the mouth.

The eyes are notably omitted from this transaction. Throughout the Bible, the eyes represent human self-determination and independence, as opposed to submission to God's voice. The eyes are the seat of rational assessment and shrewd judgment, yet it is Jesus who is our judge, not we who are to evaluate him. Our eyes are the best tools we have to observe and analyze the phenomenal world, but they are our least reliable faculty in spiritual matters. They are most susceptible to distortion by our passions, our fears and our pride.

Jesus gives us a lesson in the inappropriate use of rational assessment in John's gospel. "Now there were certain Greeks among those who came up to worship at the feast. Then they came to Philip, who was from Bethsaida of Galilee, and asked him, saying, "Sir, we wish to see Jesus." The significance of these Greeks who desired to see Jesus was not their ethnicity, but their supreme reliance on their eyes to gauge things of the spirit and of eternity. The gospels record only two encounters of Jesus with Greeks and he was not especially cordial in either case. The first meeting was with the Syro-Phoenician woman who implored Jesus to cast a demon from her daughter. We recall that Jesus rebuffed her quite curtly, saying, "Let the children be filled first, for it is not good to take the children's bread and throw it to the dogs." These Greeks who wished to see Jesus were proselytes to the Jewish faith. They submitted their request indirectly through Philip and Andrew who then relayed the request to Jesus.

Their request seems on the surface to be open, honest and reasonable. They had traveled farther than most to attend the Passover celebration and so we are inclined to grant them an earnestness in accordance with that effort. That they wished to see Jesus indicates that they had heard the message of his kingdom in their travels and were motivated at some level to investigate further. They did not simply want to observe him, but to interview him. But Jesus responded only to his two disciples, telling them, "Whoever serves me must follow me, and where I am, there will my servant be also." In the end, he did not grant these Greek pilgrims an audience. For John records that, "Jesus spoke these things, and departed, and hid himself from them."

These Greeks wished to see Jesus not to find out how they could serve and follow him, but to see if they found his teachings reasonable. Their request was not a noble one. Their intention was to interrogate Jesus, to test him, to assess whether or not they found his answers agreeable and then go away and consider their merits at their leisure. In all likelihood, they would have incorporated Jesus into some syncretistic religious philosophy of their own design, for this was the character of Greek religion. Paul encountered this same spirit in Athens:

> Then certain Epicurean and Stoic philosophers encountered him. And some said, "What does this babbler want to say?" Others said, "He seems to be a proclaimer of foreign gods," because he preached to them Jesus and the resurrection. And

they took him and brought him to the Areopagus, saying, "May we know what this new doctrine is of which you speak? For you are bringing some strange things to our ears. Therefore we want to know what these things mean." For all the Athenians and the foreigners who were there spent their time in nothing else but either to tell or to hear some new thing.

The desire of these Greeks to see Jesus illustrates that type of rational appraisal of Jesus that is misguided, unfruitful and, in fact, quite treacherous. It is this same spirit we see in Herod, that "...when he saw Jesus, he was exceedingly glad; for he had desired for a long time to see Him, because he had heard many things about Him, and he hoped to see some miracle done by Him. Then he questioned Him with many words, but He answered him nothing." Contrary to popular sentiment, Jesus did not welcome everyone, for he knew all men. He openly received those genuinely intent on following him, but he had little time for those who only wished to pick and choose what they found appealing, like a shopper squeezing fruit in the produce aisle.

Our eyes are especially unreliable to measure matters of eternity because they attach importance primarily to the immediate, and to that an importance far beyond what it deserves. Those things that are presently visible demand all their attention, and all their focus. The matters before our eyes today – our anxieties, our hopes, our joys, and our sorrows – fill their entire field of view. The psalmist speaks of the "destruction that lays waste at noonday." Under the noonday sun, our eyes cannot see the approaching sunset; therefore they assign no importance to it. They convince us that we have a surplus of time to deal with the spiritual matters that press on our hearts. Yet Jesus counsels us to "Walk while you have the light, lest darkness overtake you." The philosophers of Athens felt no urgency of passing time. They promised Paul, "We will hear you again on this matter." But he immediately left for Corinth and they never saw him again.

Subjecting Jesus to the scrutiny of our eyes is a hopeless venture because the proverb tells us, "The eyes of man are never satisfied." Those who attempt to assess Jesus with their eyes will find that there is always one more question, one more objection, one more provocative new angle to dissect (which is actually never a new angle at all). No one has ever fallen short of faith in Christ on account of a particular rational objection. If given a solution to one objection, the skeptic will just move along to another one. In the fourth century, Basil the Great observed the futility of answering one objection after another:

> The philosophers of Greece have made much ado to explain nature, and not one of their systems has remained firm and unshaken, each being overturned by its successor. It is vain to refute them; they are sufficient in themselves to destroy one another.

It should also be noted that Christians inevitably get in over their heads in disciplines where they are not qualified by training or experience to speak with proper authority. It is never wise to dabble in an unfamiliar specialty simply to prove some unrelated point. The contraction of foot-in-mouth disease is only one blunder away.

And what do we expect our eyes to conclude about Jesus? The prophet Isaiah tells us, "When we see him, there is no beauty that we should desire him." Our eyes will measure Jesus according to the priorities and values of this present world and find nothing in him that profits us today. They will dismiss his claim upon our hearts as irrelevant and ask, after the manner of Esau: "What is this birthright to me?"

Perhaps the greatest delusion of our eyes is to disguise the hardening that the passing of time works in human hearts. Our eyes present the past as a single, stationary image. The past seems motionless now, but each passing year meant everything then and those years were filled with the individual choices that formed the character of our hearts. Our eyes deceive us into thinking that we can step back into that picture at any point and direct our hearts as we could then. Yet there is a hardening that comes upon those who fail to respond to the early calls of the Spirit to follow Jesus. We fail to appreciate how irreversibly we become the sum of our unmade choices, until we suddenly discover how difficult it is to make the choice today we failed to make long ago.

Our eyes do not warn us of the danger of leaving Jesus continually under their gaze, never rejecting him, but never choosing to follow him either. Our spirits compel us to make our calling and election sure, but our eyes do not perceive this urgency. As we subject Jesus to the ongoing assessment of our eyes, we become less inclined to follow him, not more so; and this too is a delusion. We can never assume that choosing Christ will be easier later. It will always be more difficult. In the physical world, it is harder to climb the hill at 55 than it was at 25. The passage of time affects our spirits the same way. The opportunity we have to follow Christ today is poorer than yesterday's, but better than tomorrow's. It is in this sense that the writer to the Hebrews urges us, "Today, if you will hear his voice, do not harden your hearts."

The temptation to exalt our eyes to that lofty status of supreme arbiter in all matters temporal and eternal is a strong temptation because critical reasoning and empirical analysis is the glory of humanity in which we excel so easily and naturally. Because our eyes serve us so faithfully in the exploration of the visible, we suppose that that they are equally well suited to the unseen world. But our true citizenship is the spiritual realm, not the physical universe. We are spiritual beings, created to respond to spiritual revelation.

Our eyes will argue that they are well suited to judge the most essential questions of life even when they are not. The Scripture says that "Eye has not seen, nor ear heard, nor have entered into the heart of man the things which God has prepared for those who love Him. But God has revealed them to us through His Spirit." Those things God reveals through his Spirit we are to assess with our spirits. When Simon Peter confessed to Jesus, "You are the Christ, the Son of the living God." Jesus answered and said to him, "Blessed are you, Simon Bar-Jonah, for flesh and blood has not revealed this to you." When we attempt to assess the stature of Jesus using eyes fitted to the mapping of this world's terrain, they will only mislead and deceive us in the most important assessment of all.

It is in this sense that the seemingly forth-right request of these Greeks, "We wish to see Jesus," is laid bare as the misdirected course it was. Their interest in Jesus presents itself as sincere spiritual inquiry, but it is actually that restlessness that is always learning and never able to come to the knowledge of the truth. The world does not admire the dreamer who flits about aimlessly, unable to discern any goal for his life; yet it proclaims as a genius the one who describes true spirituality as a romance of the unknowable, as a search for meaning having no final destination. But doubt is a hazard in the search for spiritual truth. It is not a virtue. Society flocks to hear the philosophers of Athens, who thrill to continually tell or to hear some new thing, but scoffs at the single-minded simplicity of the Christian who sells all that he has to buy the field containing the hidden treasure.

With each passing year, our postmodern culture grows in its confidence that its eyes can adequately address all of humanity's questions of purpose, destiny and meaning. Yet Jesus did not receive these men; he did not submit himself to the critique of their eyes. In the same way, Christianity seeks validation in the philosopher's hall or the scientist's laboratory at its peril, for it will find none in these places. Therefore, Christianity must be careful not to become enamoured with gaining the approval of a society determined to examine Jesus using all the wrong tools.

6. The Battle of the Present

The Battle of the Present is Christianity's effort to exalt the benefits of the law in this life by criticising postmodern culture.

When you besiege a city for a long time, while making war against it to take it, you shall not destroy its trees by wielding an ax against them; if you can eat of them, do not cut them down to use in the siege, for the tree of the field is man's food.

Deuteronomy

There are a great many things that Jesus does for us and accomplishes in us in this present life that are very wonderful, but they all emanate from the great central truth that, in him, we have life in the age to come. When he grants us eternal life, he gives us his Spirit to live within us. And his Spirit pours forth life that expresses itself in many ways.

The Christian who has passed from death to life will be freed from shame and a poor self-image, but that is not the central truth. He will be healed and restored in his physical body, but that is not the central truth. He will be blessed materially and financially, but that is not the central truth. He will be renewed in his mind and will think more clearly, but that is not the central truth. He will have his heart filled with peace instead of anxiety and worry, but that is not the central truth. He will have wholesome relationships with his spouse and family restored, but that is not the central truth. Societies where the gospel spreads will experience order, prosperity and justice, but that is not the central truth. The central truth of the gospel is that death has been defeated and that all of these other blessings follow in the wake of Christ's victory.

During the second half of the 20th century, however, Christianity significantly transformed its message into a life-is-better-with-Jesus gospel that has lifted up these peripheral benefits of Christ above the central truth of eternal life: "If you believe in Jesus, you will be happier, more fulfilled, more focused, more secure, less conflicted and worry free." Instead of preaching Christ as the answer to the sting of death, we preach him as an elixir for a better life today with eternal life only thrown in as a by-the-way add-on. Now we understand that Christ does in fact provide many blessings in this present life. But all these things are added; they cannot be Christianity's core message of the gospel. Christianity has shifted to this better-life-now gospel in the expectation that it will attract more people seeking relief from the pressures of this world. But just the opposite is true, for the Holy Spirit does not empower this other gospel. To the extent Christianity takes up the battle of the present, several aspects of its message fall out of alignment very quickly.

First, the life-is-better-with-Jesus gospel requires that we contrast the Christian life with postmodern lifestyles. This gospel must convince people that they are essentially unhappy, unfulfilled, unfocused, insecure, conflicted and anxious. Yet many non-Christians are actually quite well adjusted as they are (while some Christians are no better off emotionally than they were before!) Christian preachers become high-pressure salesmen whose task is to sell Jesus-as-the-Great-Fixer-of-All-Present-Discomfort: "Your life is a mess, but Jesus will take over and manage it much better than you can." In accordance with this gospel, popular Christianity has increasingly propagated the myth that people are more likely to believe in Christ when their present life is going badly: If someone has lost a job, fallen ill, gotten divorced or succumbed to addiction; their trial becomes an "opportunity" for the Holy Spirit to draw them to Christ. (However, a cursory review of the plagues of Revelation confirms that the increase of calamity only drives the stubbornhearted to resist God all the more.)

Second, there are 1,001 other solutions for lifestyle improvement out there in the self-help marketplace that all claim to provide a better quality of life. Many of these are not even in conflict with Christianity, yet we feel compelled to compete with and discredit them in order to provide a greater contrast for the present benefits of the law. The Bible is not an exhaustive owner's manual on all things pertaining to the human condition. Many teachings, philosophies and disciplines completely outside of the Christian tradition provide a wide variety of physical, mental and spiritual benefits that are genuine and helpful. Christianity does not need to beat itself up every time it discovers that another religion, philosophy or discipline is doing something well that improves people's lives. When the disciples came upon a man casting out demons in the name of Jesus, they commanded him to stop, for he was a stranger, unknown to them and unfamiliar. But Jesus rebuked them for their exclusive attitude, saying, "He that is not against us is for us." The lesson here is that not all that is strange to us, unknown to us, or unfamiliar to us is against God's law. There is no arrogance so repugnant as religious arrogance that assumes that the same Spirit of God indwelling Christians cannot possibly work upon those who are outside of Christ, yet also made in the image of God.

The gospel is always good news. The mandate of Christianity toward the world is always to advocate that which is true, not to condemn that which is false. The gospel is always a positive confession. It is never a negative critique. It is never the proper role of Christianity to tear down other people's beliefs in order to exalt Jesus. When Naaman, commander of the army of the king of Syria, approached the prophet Elisha to be healed of his leprosy, Elisha instructed him, "Go and wash in the Jordan seven times, and your flesh shall be restored to you, and you shall be clean."

Elisha simply proclaimed the healing available in the Jordan River. We see nothing in this account critical of the religion of Syria. Elisha does not attack the culture, philosophies, or literature of Syria as a means of exalting the God of Israel. He does not malign the Abanah and Pharpar rivers, asserting that they are dirty, stagnant and polluted. He simply offers a remedy for Naaman's disease and leaves the choice to Naaman: to follow it not. It is a sad commentary on much of our Christian tradition that it feels loyalty to Jesus requires the desecration of all other traditions.

Third, the premise that life is better with Jesus is not necessarily true. Jesus will turn many aspects of a disciple's life in this present world upside down. A Christian will face trials, temptation, loss of status and friends, loss of control, inner conflict between the old and new natures, and spiritual disciplines that he did not experience previously. We tend to downplay this aspect of the Christian experience. People who believe in Jesus in the expectation of having a smooth road in this life often fall away very disappointed and end up worse off than before.

Fourth, the life-is-better-with-Jesus gospel leads to us promoting ourselves and our particular expression of the Christian life instead of promoting Jesus. "Look how much better I'm doing than you. I used to be as fouled up as you are, but look how much Jesus has improved me!" This message does not deliver a pleasing fragrance to society and its far-reaching impacts are very evident in society's negative attitudes toward the Christian culture today. Jesus said, "I am the way, and the truth, and the life. No one comes to the Father except through me." We can never assert that, "*We* are the way, and the truth, and the life. No one comes to the Father except through *us*."

Fifth, and perhaps most problematic, the life-is-better-with-Jesus gospel falls into the trap of offering people those things they crave rather than what they actually need. When Jesus rode triumphantly into Jerusalem on a donkey, the multitudes rejoiced and Jesus wept, for the people did not know the things that would make for their peace. They gave the proper recognition to the rightful king, but for the wrong reasons and with misplaced expectations. They praised and cheered the coming Messiah that day because they hungered for the fulfillment of their immediate earthly desires: the deliverance of Israel from the brutal occupation by Rome and the reinstatement of the Davidic kingdom in all of its glory. Jesus wept because he knew that these aspirations could never bring them peace and would ultimately lead to the destruction of Jerusalem.

How very much like these people we are! At every stage of our lives, and in many different circumstances of our lives, we are so very sure of what things will bring us peace. We arrive at certain critical junctures of our lives where we are absolutely certain that our greatest need is that thing which will satisfy my most immediate appetite. "If I can only just get this one thing, I will be at peace." The 10-year old needs the latest toy or gadget that all the other kids have. The teenager will absolutely die if she cannot get a date with that cute guy in her English class. A few years later, marriage and the right career choice are the essential keys to peace. Then it is the perfect job and the choice house in the right part of town. Then, having achieved the other things, we spend our later years chasing promotions and building retirement packages.

At every point along the way, we are tempted by the illusion that the crest of the next horizon will be the ultimate milestone of my life journey. And yet how quickly that great prize that occupied our entire vision just a moment ago loses its lustre after we attain it. We soon realize, as we have realized on previous occasions, that it really didn't deliver that lasting peace it promised. For we will never find our peace in our accomplishments. The Preacher considers our efforts in this life and declares in Ecclesiastes, "All the labor of man is for his mouth, and yet the soul is not satisfied." Now the labor of man is an honorable endeavor, for God made the mouth just as he created the soul. It is God's pleasure that our mouths be satisfied with the accomplishments of this life. But the delights of the mouth do not satisfy the soul, and herein lies the stumbling of the multitudes that first Palm Sunday. For they imagined that they would find peace for their souls in the liberation of their land from Roman oppression.

Had Jesus chosen to grant the people what they sought, he could have overthrown Rome that very day. Scholars estimate that there were perhaps 3,000 people cheering him that day. He could have rallied them against the Roman garrison in Jerusalem, taken the city by surprise, put Pilate and all his officers to the sword and set up his throne in the temple.

Before Rome had time to react, the rebellion would have spread throughout Judea, and the whole land liberated from the Roman tyranny. But we are all too familiar with new governments supplanting old governments. We see the celebrations of the victors, the promises of justice and prosperity; and then, predictably, we see the new government come to look very much like the old one. For any government will quickly take on the character of its citizens. But these are not the things that make for our peace. This was not the first time Jesus had opportunity to claim an earthly kingdom. Satan made the same offer when he tempted Jesus in the wilderness. Jesus rejected it then and he rejects it here. For his objective was something much larger, more lasting and infinitely more satisfying.

Jesus had an appointment from which he would not be deterred. The multitudes, Satan, even his disciples all enticed him to settle for something less. But Luke tells us that Jesus set his face to go to Jerusalem and keep this appointment. It was the work for which he had been sent and he would not be moved from his course. Had Jesus yielded to these temptations, he could have avoided this appointment and still have accomplished many things that would have placed him among the great figures of history. He could have led great liberating armies, overthrown tyrants, healed tens of thousands and written volumes of books amplifying his teachings. He could have established schools and training centers. But all these were not the purpose for which he was sent.

Many people who fail to find peace in their accomplishments attempt to find peace in their service. Surely here is the key to my peace! I will pour my energy into service to the weak, to the oppressed, to those whose voice is not heard. After all, devoting my life to meeting the needs of others certainly carries a higher moral tone than pursuing my own accomplishments. But neither will service bring us our peace because the tides of success and failure ebb and flow in all human affairs. Sometimes the goodness, the humility and the self-sacrifice of the human spirit we observe in our brothers and sisters will fill our hearts with admiration and hope. And then, in the next moment, the cruelty, the callousness and the depravity of one human being to another will send us reeling in horror.

Many people enter public service through the helping professions hoping to resolve the unanswered questions of peace and satisfaction in their own souls as they reach out to others. But they do not find their peace in such work, for they discover, as Jesus foretold, that, "The poor you will always have with you." Some wrongs will be put right, but new evils will replace them. Some will be healed, but many more will fall sick. As worthy a fight as this is, the ministry of mercy and compassion is a battle that will have no final conclusion in this world.

The struggle against oppression, poverty and injustice is the right and proper labor of Christianity. Both the Old and New Testament prophets command the people of God to fight injustice and inequality wherever and in whatever form it is found: whether it is an impoverished population persecuted by a dictator, the denial of human rights, the exploitation of people or the environment through human greed or any other expression of evil. We fight this fight not because we have weighed the odds of success and calculated our chances of winning. But we fight because every individual on whose behalf we struggle is created in the image of God and is deserving of the dignity of that status.

We would be greatly mistaken if we concluded that Jesus had no compassion for the multitudes that celebrated his arrival in Jerusalem that Palm Sunday. He fully understood what the Jews suffered under Rome and the cruel tyranny of Pontius Pilate and Herod. But on this day, he passed them by, for their greatest desire for present relief was not their most pressing need. The human heart is blatantly fickle in this matter of finding our peace. It is in our natures, no matter how many dilemmas are resolved in our lives, to run immediately to the next one and declare it to be the final objective. For when we ground our peace in the affairs of this world, it is a peace that will only endure until the next crisis appears.

If we want to understand the things that make for our peace, we need to accept first of all that we are spiritual beings who reside in these perishable bodies for only a very brief moment. We naturally assume just the opposite: that our identity is essentially physical with some nebulous component of spirit that becomes important when we die, but that really doesn't amount to anything now. Once we grasp this reality of our spiritual natures, we can better appreciate the fact that the things that make for our peace are spiritual. We can also appreciate the incongruity of a spiritual creature attempting to ground his peace in the changing and uncertain currents of this world. And so Jesus looked upon the multitudes and he wept, for they did not comprehend their need, or the work that he must complete at Golgotha. For Jesus had an appointment on Good Friday with a Roman cross. And it is in this appointment that we discover the things that make for our peace.

It is the peace that flows from the cross that equips us to minister to the hurts and needs and yearnings of this present world. Our peace is anchored in eternity through Christ's surrender of himself to the cross. And that peace is the reference point that empowers us to reach out to the practical, here-and-now needs of this present world. God invites us to enjoy the good and pleasant labors of this world. But these accomplishments are not the things that make for our peace. God also calls us to minister to the hurts and injustices that oppress our brothers and sisters in this world. But neither is our service that which makes for our peace. It is required of us that we make our peace with God before we can become peacemakers in this world.

Jesus passed by the multitudes that first Palm Sunday and he did not grant them the deliverance they hoped for. In the same way, he will sometimes pass by you and me without addressing that pain that we feel most sharply today. And when he does this, do not immediately assume that he is slow, or deaf or blind. But consider that he may be leading us to rediscover the things that make for our peace, things that, from time to time in the mad rush of this life, become hidden from our eyes. The world demands instant relief from the miseries, the stresses and the contradictions of this life. Jesus certainly provides this relief, but Christianity's challenge is to resist the temptation to proclaim a gospel that makes this present life the core of its message. More than ever before in this materialistic and postmodern culture, Christianity must leave the battle of the present to those who only believe in the present. Its answer to those who demand that Christianity take up that battle must be that its first and foremost duty is to address the question of eternity.

7. The Battle of the World

The Battle of the World is Christianity's reactionary application of the law to the postmodern agenda.

Those skilled in war bring the enemy to the field of battle and are not brought there by him.

Sun Tzu

As the influence of a biblically-oriented perspective has diminished over the last generation, we have seen a corresponding rise of the "Christian counterpoint" refuting postmodern views on contemporary issues and events. Such an editorial voice was hardly necessary in a society that knew only a Judeo-Christian worldview, for there was no significant opposition to provide any contrasting opinion. Today, however, we see "Christian" positions published on every hot-button issue of the day, whether political, economic, ethical, environmental or social. Christianity is increasingly driven to demonstrate its relevance to current affairs through declaring the law's application to specific headline issues. Christian denominations and organizations of every stripe cannot resist issuing press releases in response to every news item that comes across the wire, setting forth "God's view" on the matter. There are a number of reasons why this practice is unsound and unproductive.

First, we fail to appreciate how strongly our own local horizons and biases influence our present opinions. In the majority of cases, the passage of time reveals how short sighted our pronouncements were. Trace any particular issue back through the history of Christian thought—even ten or twenty years—and you will see how strongly a generation's particular cultural lenses color its views.

Second, one of the distinctive elements of the Bible is that each of its central teachings is matched with a contrasting viewpoint. For example, God predetermines my path, but also calls me to choose my way. Money is a blessing, yet the love of money is the root of all evil. We are to judge wisely, but we are also warned to judge not. A Christian is a saint as well as a sinner. Our task is not to reconcile these opposites, but to wrestle with them and allow their tensions to stand. It is in our wrestling with these difficult counterpoints that the Holy Spirit teaches us how to work out God's wisdom in the real situation of our lives. The Spirit may legitimately lead two people in opposite directions on the same question! Our editorial positions almost always commit the error of embracing one truth at the expense of ignoring its complement.

Third, the government of creation will not allow the government of redemption to impose the grid of the law over its affairs (See Chapter 2 on the relationship between these two governments). A Christian may participate in the government of creation as a citizen of that government, but he must do so wisely and circumspectly. He can advocate for justice, creation wisdom and other elements of common agreement; but he may not appeal to God's absolute law without incurring an immediate negative reaction. A lawless culture will forcefully reject any declaration of objective law originating outside of its own self-determination.

Fourth, Jesus provided the example of avoiding the battlefields the world chooses.

When faced with the question, "Is it lawful to pay taxes to Caesar, or not?" he discerned that it was designed to put him in the wrong whichever answer he gave. The Pharisees demanded that Jesus declare himself as either a Jewish zealot or a Roman collaborator, but he refused to cooperate. He said to them, in effect, "my categories are my own and I don't submit to yours." We are only too happy to offer unqualified answers to the question, "What is lawful?" where Jesus himself would not venture to speak. This society's categories are not the gospel's categories. The post-modern world declares to Christianity what labels it must choose. It attempts to dictate to Christianity what essential issues and divisions and categories it must use to define its message. But we can never forget that the call to follow Jesus requires that *we* join Jesus. Jesus does not join *our* causes and categories.

The dramatic conversion of Saul of Tarsus provides us with a striking lesson of a man who found his own categories of relevance demolished when a very relevant God interrupted his agenda. We find much to admire in Saul as he traveled to Damascus. He was a man of unshakeable determination and conviction. He hungered after righteousness and sought to enforce it as best he knew how. He turned his convictions into action without regard for his own safety or welfare. But Saul's faults are equally evident. And it is because of these that God chooses him, just as God chooses each of us for our weaknesses rather than because of our strengths. Saul's view of God was forged out of his own priorities, expectations and experience. He professed to act for God, but he did not know God. And so it was that Saul's meeting with God was something very different than he expected.

> Then Saul, still breathing threats and murder against the disciples of the Lord, went to the high priest and asked letters from him to the synagogues of Damascus, so that if he found any who were of the Way, whether men or women, he might bring them bound to Jerusalem. As he journeyed he came near Damascus, and suddenly a light shone around him from heaven. Then he fell to the ground, and heard a voice saying to him, "Saul, Saul, why are you persecuting me?" And he said, "Who are you, Lord?" Then the Lord said, "I am Jesus, whom you are persecuting. It is hard for you to kick against the goads."

So he, trembling and astonished, said, "Lord, what do you want me to do?" Then the Lord said to him, "Arise and go into the city, and you will be told what you must do." And the men who journeyed with him stood speechless, hearing a voice but seeing no one. Then Saul arose from the ground, and when his eyes were opened he saw no one. But they led him by the hand and brought him into Damascus. And he was three days without sight, and neither ate nor drank.

The immediate effect on Saul of the light from heaven was not illumination, but blindness. Let us be careful not to miss this central statement in the account of Saul's conversion, for it is a foundational theme running through the entire Bible. The declaration I speak of is God's judgment on the independence, wilful determination and self-direction of his people. The light from heaven struck Saul blind and he persisted in this condition for three days. Saul's eyes symbolize that wilful self-determination that God must subdue before we can become suitable vessels for accomplishing his purposes.

In Chapter 5, I spoke of the eyes as representing our exaltation of natural reason over spiritual discernment. Yet they can also refer to human self-direction and independence contrasted against God's immediate guidance and direction. It is through our eyes that we strive to assert our own ways and desires over God's direction and provision. In the Garden of Eden, the woman saw that the tree was good for food, that it was pleasant to the eyes. Lot lifted his eyes and saw all the plain of Jordan and chose the well-watered land of Sodom and Gomorrah that would lead to his family's ruin. The final summary verse of the Book of Judges laments, "In those days there was no king in Israel; everyone did what was right in his own eyes." Samuel first trusted in his eyes to select Eliab as God's anointed until the voice of the Lord revealed that David was to be Israel's king. John warns us against the lust of the eyes that leads us to pursue prideful independence from God.

If you had to choose between your sight and your hearing, which would you select? Most of us would unhesitatingly choose our eyes. For it is with our eyes that we assess the world around us and do our business within it. But the proper choice for the Christian must be his ears. For if we do not hear the voice of God, then we are absolutely cast adrift to our own devices. Our ears represent an attitude of submission to the will and voice of God. It is our ears that allow us to hear God call us individually by our names, provide guidance and comfort, and impart his wisdom. God's people are to move and act and choose only as they hear from God.

The manner of Saul's conversion teaches us that the purpose of light from heaven is not to give us an enlightened view of this world or of ourselves. But its purpose is to reveal the God who cannot be known until he makes himself known. This was not a light that afforded Saul a better understanding of the world he already knew. It was a light that shattered everything he had thought was true, certain and immovable. It was not a light that showed Saul how to build on his own priorities and objectives. It was a light that cast him to the ground and completely destroyed his orientation to all that he had previously known.

When God appeared in his glory to Isaiah, the prophet declared, "I am undone." The Hebrew word for "undone" means "to be destroyed" or "to be laid waste." Both the prophet Isaiah and Saul of Tarsus had firm principles, convictions and motives. They were confident of their places in the world and what things must be done and said on God's behalf. They had their list of questions, their complaints, their categories, their strong opinions about what critical issues of the day the law needed to address. But when God himself appeared, their entire framework of reality was burned up in an instant. God's glory cast them to the ground, both literally and in every other sense.

Saul's conversion also illustrates the doctrine of prevenient grace, which is the teaching that, before a person can seek God, God must first have sought the person. The familiar refrain, "I saw the light" as a metaphor for the experience of Christian conversion is derived from Saul's conversion. But the revelation of God is a not a light that illuminates our view of the world. It is a light that, by its stunning brilliance, confounds, overwhelms, humbles, disorients, and leaves us wondering if we ever knew anything before that moment of encounter with the living God.

And so when the light from heaven cast Saul to the ground, God disabled Saul's sight so that he would be forced to hear. And in this condition, helpless, prostrate on the ground and blind, he was ready to begin his service to Jesus. Out of all his great learning, the most profound thing he could say was, "Who are you, Lord?" If we amplified Saul's question a bit it would run something like this: "I know what my teachers have taught me, but who are you? I know what my books have taught me, but who are you? I know what my traditions have taught me, but who are you?"

And then Saul asks a second question: "What do you want me to do?" I wonder if we have become too sophisticated to ask such a question. It is a humiliating thing to admit that we must ask God what he would have us do. In contrast, postmodern society is so definite in its purposes; so sure of what things must be done to address the critical priorities of the day. Until Christianity humbles itself to ask these questions of God, it can never attain to its true purpose and calling in this world.

It is a tremendous temptation to be drawn away by the energy of self-determination that characterizes postmodern culture. We feel the thrill of the flesh when we draw from our own experience, our own convictions, our own beliefs, our own strategies and solutions to declare, "This is the will of God." We march forward in perfect confidence that our priorities are God's priorities. Every army goes to war in the name of God. Every cause declares in all conviction that God is surely aligned with our cause. But the counsels of God do not take their bearings from the affairs of this world.

Christianity can only fulfil its prophetic mandate in a postmodern world if it first turns a blind eye toward its demands. Hear me very carefully on this point. I do not mean that we are to ignore society's *cry*, but that we must not use society's *priorities* as our reference points. Loving parents diligently hear and attend to the needs of their children, but they do not gratify every desire, nor do they address every need their children bring to the table. The Old Testament prophets certainly had their own views and opinions, but they were compelled to proclaim only the word of the Lord delivered to them. To the degree that Christianity stops listening to God it surrenders its prophetic calling to other cultural forces.

Israel demanded a king so that it could be like all the nations. In the same way, Christianity is too often content to simply apply the law to the priorities postmodern culture declares. Instead of following Christ, the government of redemption only reacts to the government of creation. The real tragedy in this is that it's so predictable. God wants to make Christians a people like no other people. Peter calls Christians a peculiar people, a people who are strangers in this world. Yet all we want to do is mirror a "sanctified" reflection of the priorities the world has predetermined for us. When Nehemiah was rebuilding the walls of Jerusalem, the local political leaders came around and tried to recruit him to their purposes, saying, "Come, let us meet together." But Nehemiah responded, saying, "I am doing a great work, so that I cannot come down. Why should the work cease while I leave it and go down to you?" Christianity's answer to the world should always be Nehemiah's response: "We are doing a great work and cannot come down. You are welcome to come up and join us, but we cannot come down."

Instead, like Saul on the road to Damascus, Christianity strives to accomplish the righteousness of God using what is known, familiar and manageable. We would force God to conform to the immediate issues of our day. We are so quick to presume that society's priorities are God's priorities. But when the light from heaven confronts us, it does not take our theologies, our politics, our philosophies, our convictions and renovate them into new and improved versions; but God undoes us.

One of the most liberating and healthy things we can learn about God is that he has an identity and personality apart from his creation's needs and expectations. After Joshua led Israel across the Jordan River, the angel of the Lord appeared to him as a man with his sword drawn in His hand. And Joshua went to Him and said to Him, "Are you for us or for our adversaries?" And the angel of the Lord said, "No, but as Commander of the army of the Lord I have now come." Do you know that God's personality and identity does not revolve around our priorities and the burning issues of our day? What would we think of a parent whose only identity is found through chasing after every demand of clamouring children? When we are children, we see our parents only through the lens of our own immediate needs. Our parents exist only to facilitate our daily expectations and desires. But as we mature, we come to realize that our parents actually had lives and identities and purposes before we were born. The worst mistake parents can make is to allow their own identities to be consumed by the priorities of their children. God is a wise parent and he does not allow this to happen.

As Saul traveled on the road to Damascus, his heart full of malice and violence, his passion was for the righteousness of God. He attempted to execute God's righteousness on his own terms. And yet his concept of God was skewed and incomplete. Saul had a very airtight theology, but his theology lacked the reality of encounter with the living God. And then the light from heaven turned his world upside down. He was suddenly confronted with a very complete God and a very inadequate theology (which is, in fact, a very good place to be). Saul had no doubt that he was in the very presence of God, and he knew also that his agenda and his priorities were undone.

It is essential that Christianity continually come to God with Saul's two questions: "Who are you, Lord" and "What do you want me to do?" If it does, it will discover a God who is really a very proactive and relevant person. It will also discover that God is quite capable of revealing his own horizons and accomplishing his purposes on his schedule.

8. The Battle of the Law

The Battle of the Law is Christianity's insistence on presenting the gospel exclusively in terms of a legal reconciliation with God.

> *...I have made myself a servant to all, that I might win the more; and to the Jews I became as a Jew, that I might win Jews; to those who are under the law, as under the law, that I might win those who are under the law; to those who are without law, as without law (not being without law toward God, but under law toward Christ), that I might win those who are without law...*
>
> *1 Corinthians*

The apostles realized the need to communicate the gospel to two radically different worldviews: those under the law and those without the law. Jews had the Law of Moses that provided a context for understanding the necessity of a reconciliation between the Lawgiver and the lawbreaker. Gentiles, however, had a relativistic worldview that knew nothing of any legal alienation from God requiring reconciliation. As I have already mentioned in the first chapter, 21st-century society fits predominantly into this relativistic, lawless category. People who are "without the law" do not easily relate to the concept that they are legally separated from God.

It is significant, therefore, to consider that Christianity's predominant presentation of the good news today is that Christ died to solve a legal problem; that is, to take away the penalty for sin. Sin is understood biblically as "falling short of a fixed standard" or "missing the mark" and constitutes a legal separation between the Lawmaker and the lawbreaker. The presentation of the gospel in these terms connected very well with the culture of forty years ago that was under the law. However, it faces a major hurdle in the new society. In a lawless culture where fixed standards are not recognized, sin can find no mark to miss; therefore it ceases to have any significance. Sin is not a perceived problem in a postmodern society, for as Paul says, "I would not have known sin except through the law." For example, consider that the state of Montana had no speed limits on its highways until 1999. In such an environment, speeding might be a safety problem, but it is not a legal problem. An announcement that the governor is forgiving speeding fines would hardly rate as good news! Presenting the gospel from a perspective of the legal problem of sin assumes that the hearer already views sin as lawbreaking. But a lawless society does not see sin as a problem. And if there is no perceived problem, then the gospel is not good news.

The 'bad news' of humanity's legal separation from God that Christianity typically uses to frame the gospel is theologically correct, but it is a poor access point to the gospel for a culture that is without the law. It is, in fact, very distracting from the task at hand: communicating the single point that Jesus Christ is good news. A good salesman focuses exclusively on his customer's felt needs. This wise salesman realizes that trying to convince a customer he has a need of which he is unaware is an uphill, low-percentage battle. He avoids such arguments. He tells the truth about his product, but he says no more than is necessary to close the sale. He doesn't describe everything he knows about the product. He doesn't answer objections that don't occur to the customer. He knows that the customer will be satisfied with his product, so he focuses exclusively on those points that will convince the customer to buy it.

The premise of the gospel being "good news," presupposes a problem to be solved. But exactly what problem does the gospel solve? This question is answered when we realize that the ultimate problem the gospel addresses is not sin, but death, "...when desire has conceived, it gives birth to sin; and sin, when it is full-grown, brings forth death." Death is a bitter and painful reality to accept because Ecclesiastes tells us that God has put eternity in our hearts. Deep down, every one of us knows that we're not supposed to die. God created us as eternal creatures. And so we find no shortage of religions and philosophies that attempt to make sense out of the absurdity of a life that ends inexplicably in death:

- Hinduism teaches the delusion of reincarnation; that death is just a transition to a subsequent appearance in this world, which will be followed by still more appearances. So in this way, death is actually a friend that takes this life away for a better one next time around.

- Everyday in the headlines, we read of religious fanatics who regard murder/suicide as a doorway to great honor in an afterlife; that if you choose to die in this particular way, death will reward you.

- In the last century, communism tried to deal with death by minimizing the individual's identity and magnifying the collective glory of the proletariat masses. If a person fully devoted himself to the communist cause, then he would never really die, but would live on in the glorious spirit of the revolution.

- Hedonism teaches that the basic purpose of life is to indulge in the sensual pleasures of youth to the maximum extent possible. Death actually does us a service by taking us out when our energies start to fade.

- Postmodernism holds that death is simply a natural process in a materialistic universe that must be stoically accepted. Life and the inevitable death that follows are really just biological processes. There's no benefit in entertaining any grief or regret, because death is just nature's cycling of the physical elements.

It is far preferable to present the good news of Jesus Christ as the answer to the tragedy of death that is universally recognized and avoid arguing about the problem of sin with those who do not have the law. The essence of the gospel is found in the very familiar passage, "For God so loved the world that He gave His only begotten Son, that whoever believes in Him should not perish but have everlasting life." We see here that the "problem" is perishing, or death, and the relief Jesus provides is everlasting life. Jesus Christ came into the world to relieve the "sting of death." This is the gospel we are to proclaim. This message has a distinct element that makes it especially effective. That is, the problem is universal or, as my friend George puts it, "Everybody has the same bus ticket; it's only a question of when it gets punched." This message allows no preliminary arguments that need to be won before proceeding to the main point. No one can say, "Sorry, that condition doesn't apply to me. I'm not going to die."

The gospel is only good news if it offers relief from some bad news that is already recognized.

Unfortunately, because Christianity insists on packaging its gospel message in the legal problem of sin, postmodernism has a very hard time getting past the wrapping paper. 21st-century Christianity erroneously believes that it has to bring people under the law as a prerequisite to their delivery from the curse of the law! It will therefore come as a surprise to many Christians that the Bible does not require people to confess their sin as a condition of gaining eternal life (see Chapter 4 on this point). When we examine the faith statements the New Testament requires to obtain eternal life, we find much more basic confessions. Jesus said, "He who believes in the Son has everlasting life;" and, again, "He who hears my word and believes in Him who sent me has everlasting life." The Ethiopian eunuch confessed simply, "I believe that Jesus Christ is the Son of God." John testifies, "Whoever believes that Jesus is the Christ is born of God."

The gospel in its essence is the message that Jesus freely offers me eternal life in the place of death. It is true that he died on the cross to remove the legal barrier to me receiving this gift. However, Christ's payment of the penalty for my lawbreaking *is not the gift itself*—it is the legal transaction that makes the gift possible. Christ does not offer me the gift of eternal life because his payment of my penalty for lawbreaking compels him to do so. He offers me this gift willingly because he loves me and wants me to live with him forever. This is the gospel Christianity is to proclaim.

Here is an illustration to demonstrate my point. Suppose I am fatally ill with a disease having no known cure. Then one day my doctor informs me that he has acquired a new medicine that will completely heal me with a single dose. I only need to sign a consent form to allow him to administer the treatment, which I readily do. I then receive the medicine and make a complete recovery. I only learn afterward that my dosage cost $10,000,000. A complete stranger heard of my plight, took pity on me and sold everything he had to purchase one dosage of my life-giving medicine. The point of this illustration is that, at the moment of my consent, my cure did not depend on me knowing the price of the medicine and how the price was paid. I only needed to give assent to the treatment in order to receive its benefit. The "good news" was the medicine offered to me. The sacrificial payment of $10,000,000 was the transaction that made the good news possible.

This is a critical distinction for Christianity to embrace as it relates to a postmodern culture. God only requires that a person believe in Jesus Christ for the gift of eternal life, not that he believe rightly about his own sin. Access to the forgiveness of sins is a subsequent benefit of receiving eternal live, only available *after* one gains eternal life. Paul lays out this sequence of transactions: "He has delivered us from the power of darkness and conveyed us into the kingdom of the Son of His love, in whom we have redemption through His blood, the forgiveness of sins." People do not first require a theological overview of redemption, reconciliation and justification in order to believe in Jesus for eternal life. While these transactions between the Father and the Son have made his confession of faith possible, they are matters of the law to be unfolded to the new disciple later, after he receives the gift of eternal life.

Another difficulty with a gospel message based on the problem of sin is that the law is unnecessarily brought into view, for "the strength of sin is the law." Speaking generally, Christians have a muddled understanding of the distinct role of each person of the Trinity with regard to the law. The Father declares the law, the Spirit convicts of breaking the law, but the Son came only to fulfill the law. He came not to judge, but to save. Jesus did not send his disciples forth to proclaim the law. Christians do not represent either the Father to proclaim the law or the Spirit to convict of breaking the law. Christians are emissaries only of the Son, to proclaim the life he offers to the world. A postmodern society will not tolerate Christianity's imposition of the law. It will not tolerate a presentation of the gospel that says, "You must believe in the Son because you have broken the Father's law." Such packaging of the gospel is unnecessary, counterproductive and generally devoid of fruit. Christianity gets very little mileage out of preaching the law to this present culture.

Christianity should be perfectly clear in its own mind, therefore, that the essence and central truth of the good news of Jesus Christ is that he died and was raised again to life in order to overturn the curse of death; that those who believe in him will receive everlasting life. Where it encounters those under the law, Christianity can certainly appeal to the problem of sin and the separation from God it imposes. But this legal argument is a tool necessarily restricted to those having the law. It is not the gospel message itself. Christianity brings a distinctive message that no one else can bring to a world under the curse of death. And it needs to be ever watchful that it does not allow other arguments concerning the law, theologically correct as they may be, to overshadow this one central truth: that whoever believes in Jesus "should not perish but have eternal life."

9. The Battle of Being Right

The Battle of Being Right is Christianity's preoccupation with exposing the errors of lawlessness.

To the angel of the Church of Ephesus write, "I know your works, your labor, your patience, and that you cannot bear those who are evil. And you have tested those who say they are apostles and are not, and have found them liars; and you have persevered and have patience, and have labored for My name's sake and have not become weary. Nevertheless I have this against you, that you have left your first love. Remember therefore from where you have fallen; repent and do the first works, or else I will come to you quickly and remove your lampstand from its place-unless you repent. But this you have, that you hate the deeds of the Nicolaitans, which I also hate."

Revelation

The greatest dangers in the Christian life are those that ensnare us so slowly and quietly that we hardly notice their advance. They encircle and entangle us a millimeter at a time. Like staring at the hour hand of a clock, we do not notice their relentless shifting and repositioning in our lives. The church at Ephesus did not leave its first love through a conscious decision on any particular day that could be distinguished from a thousand days that preceded it. But over a long period of time, its orientation had shifted from being a vibrant, living love affair with Jesus to something very different, very stale and very unattractive. The church at Ephesus had become a culture of opposition, where its primary identification had shifted from the life it affirmed to the lawlessness it opposed.

We often recognize this condition in others. It is characterized by guardedness, cynicism, reserve, suspicion, reactionary defensiveness and often a certain measure of bitterness. The condition is also marked by the absence of lightness, joy, passion, spontaneity and fullness. These people are the self-appointed guardians of that which is safe, manageable and predictable. They bear the scars of injuries suffered in old battles, many of which have never healed properly. They oppose the darkness, but take no joy in the light. They refute error, but no longer delight in truth. They keep an orderly house, but their home is devoid of warmth.

Ephesus had assumed a role that is a necessary and proper one for Christianity, but which can never serve as its essential identity. Certainly Christianity must always oppose evil and falsehood in its own house if its spiritual life is to be preserved, but that struggle is not the life itself. The people at Ephesus lost track of this distinction. Martha's work in the kitchen was proper and necessary, but it was not the focal point of the gathering. She forgot why she was there while Mary celebrated Jesus' visit to their home. God confronted the church at Ephesus with its deficiency because his love toward us is not blind. He does not say, "As many as I love I commend," but, "As many as I love, I rebuke and chasten." If we are to grow into our full potential in Christ, it is more important that we discover our faults than our virtues.

In Matthew's gospel, Jesus taught a fundamental principle about opposing evil.

When an unclean spirit goes out of a man, he goes through dry places, seeking rest, and finds none. Then he says, 'I will return to my house from which I came.' And when he comes, he finds it empty, swept, and put in order. Then he goes and takes with him seven other spirits more wicked than himself, and they enter and dwell there; and the last state of that man is worse than the first.

This lesson teaches us that the absence of evil is not a thing in itself. It has no substance or weight that can sustain the life of the household. The owner had done well to evict the evil spirit. He had then swept the house and put everything in order. But there were no occupants and therefore no life. When the evil spirit returned, he found only emptiness, only a vacuum.

The church at Ephesus wouldn't have known what to do without its supporting cast of enemies. Like NATO after the collapse of the Soviet Union, it had no life apart from fighting the evildoers, the false apostles and the Nicolaitans. It was like the retiree who had done nothing for the last forty years except struggle to reach retirement. He had worked to pay the bills, pay off the house, get the kids through college, and build his retirement fund. And then, with all his lifelong opponents vanquished, he has no idea what to do with his sixteen waking hours every day.

A healthy Christianity draws its life from its love of Jesus. It recognizes its enemies, but does not rely on them for its identity and purpose. Its life flows from the indwelling Holy Spirit. That life is a fountain bringing refreshment to all who draw near. The New Testament picture of Christ and his church is that of the bridegroom and his bride. The bride rejoices in the bridegroom, their marriage, and the home they have together.

What is the essence of a marriage? Is it the absence of infidelity? Is it material provision? Is it the legal fulfillment of a signed contract? No: it is the intimacy of being in love and growing in that love. All these other things flow out of the love of the bride and the bridegroom toward each other. But Ephesus had left its first love. So serious was the error of Ephesus that God warns them to repent or risk having their lampstand removed. The lampstand is synonymous with God's abiding presence and continued blessing on our labors. For a Christianity that has fallen out of love with Jesus has lost its reason for existence. When its love toward Jesus grows cold, Christianity descends into a sterile, forbidding moralism.

In a former pastorate, I served a congregation that suffered from this condition. The founding families of this church had all splintered off from larger denominational structures. A few months into my appointment, I began to understand the personality of this congregation. Their primary focus was on the traditions, the terminology, the worship styles, and the leadership structures they were determined to avoid. They were crystal clear about all they opposed. This was their point of unity. Unfortunately, they were quite foggy about what they wanted to *pursue* and exactly what they stood *for*.

Such was the verdict over Ephesus. Yes, they were diligent, patient and hardworking. But they had grounded their identity in those things they opposed, the teachings they refuted, and the errors they rebuked. They were quick to observe when someone else was off balance, but did not venture out on to the dance floor themselves. They were Right, but they were no longer true; and there is all the difference in the world between the two.

We who comprise the body of Christ are to be people of the truth, for "...he who does the truth comes to the light, that his deeds may be clearly seen, that they have been done in God." Truth is not what one believes, but what one does. All too often we focus on simply being Right. The difference can be that of giving off a pleasing aroma as opposed to a wretched stench. The biblical concept of truth carries the idea of something being genuine rather than just a façade of correctness. A person is of the truth not simply because he believes God said to visit orphans and widows in their affliction, but because he actually does it. He is genuine. Another aspect of biblical truth is that it is efficacious; that is, it actually accomplishes its stated purpose. Jesus declared himself to be the truth not because he came from the Father, but because he did his Father's will. Because the Spirit is truth, it bears witness. Truth does not merely inform, but it sets free those who abide in it.

In contrast, being Right has none of these attributes. It is a cloak for fear, arrogance, pride and lovelessness. The task of theology becomes a largely abstract contest to build a bigger and better exposition of the law. Jesus confronted a group of Jews over the attitude of being Right, "You search the Scriptures because you think that in them you have eternal life." The activity involved in developing and maintaining our Rightness is busywork that insulates us from the harsh reality that we are accomplishing little that will endure into eternity.

What typically happens to lead Christians into this error is a confrontation with their own ineffectiveness. There could be any one of a hundred reasons for this ineffectiveness, but the point is that they realize that they are not transforming the world around them. In fact, they are watching society decline before their eyes and feel powerless to slow the awful momentum. It is precisely in the midst of this attitude that Christianity is susceptible to making a subtle shift in its mission. Being painfully aware that it is losing the game of transforming society, it quietly folds up *Spread the Gospel* and takes up a new game – *Being Right*. In *Being Right*, the point of the game is for Christianity to prove (mainly to itself) that all of its views and positions are Right, as opposed to all contradicting views (which are, of course, Wrong). This goal is achieved through producing massive quantities of arguments, papers, editorials and sermons all explaining and re-explaining and defending and re-defending their Rightness.

Being Right is much more fun to play for a number of reasons. First, Christianity can never lose at this game because there is no way of keeping score. In fact, the game is especially enjoyable if no opponent shows up, although opponents are occasionally allowed. Second, Christianity's objective in *Being Right* is not to invite the world to believe the gospel, but rather to confirm to itself again and again that it is Right and they are Wrong. (This element is a decided 'improvement' over *Spread the Gospel*!) Third, *Being Right* is basically a theoretical game. Everyone understands that our Right views will never be tried and tested by the Wrong majority who would clearly benefit so tremendously if they simply put our Right views into practice.

What this shift from *Spread the Gospel* to *Being Right* represents is a movement of Christianity from a salt-in-the-world to a fortress-against-the-world mentality. Without realizing it, Christianity falls into an illusory posture where it sees the attainment of a well-developed and well-defended system of Rightness as being in itself the work of the gospel. Yet it is not. At the final Day there will be no virtue in having manned the "at-least-we-were-right" watchtower.

The temptation to fight the battle of *Being Right* is understandable, for 21st-century Christianity still remembers its influential stature in the 20th century. From this perspective, it seems so compelling that Christianity should make every effort to cast down its critics now, while some glowing ember of its past glory in the West remains. But this urge to take up the sword is soulish and does not arise from the prompting of the Spirit. We live in a time when every opponent of the law capable of throwing a brick is acclaimed a genius for destroying that which he has no capacity to replace. Flesh and blood cannot hope to push back against this postmodern storm.

Christianity's former designation as society's lawgiver is passed away and will not be restored, for it was many centuries in the making. The building that collapses in a minute is not replaced in a day, or even in a month. The conclusion then is not that Christianity's role in Western culture is ended; but that whatever influence it retains in a postmodern society certainly will not resemble its past. To the extent it pursues a public profile in the 21st century, Christianity must accept a minority role in a pluralistic setting.

The tragedy in waging the battle of *Being Right* is not the loss of the battle itself, for some lost battles have their vindication in the final balance of victory. But in this case, *Being Right* is the wrong battle because even victory bears no fruit. Jesus did not send entrust us with his gospel for the purpose of winning debates and proving our opponents wrong. The real tragedy of playing *Being Right* is the misplaced time and effort diverted from Christianity's singular obligation to love the Lord our God with all our heart, all our mind and all our soul.

10. The Battle of the Future

The Battle of the Future is Christianity's expectation that those without the law will come into the visible community of the law.

When we consider the evangelistic methods of Jesus, we can hardly escape the conclusion that he essentially responded to the present opportunities and appointments his Father brought to him. Jesus taught from the subjects and contexts he discovered day by day. He had a clear goal and purpose, but no fixed strategy for spreading the gospel. He did not bring a canned presentation of teachings to his ministry. Rather, he took his cue from the questions and demands of individuals he encountered in the moment. Jesus started from an individual's perceived need and moved into matters of eternity from that point. His disciples were continually dismayed at how their Master failed to pursue high-profile people who could have carried his message into the mainstreams of influence, yet inexplicably lingered with some disreputable 'nobody' who appeared out of nowhere. In every respect he lived out his own counsel, "...do not worry about tomorrow, for tomorrow will worry about its own things. Sufficient for the day is its own trouble."

If we are to take seriously Jesus' opportunity-oriented ministry style as being a model for our own, we need to accept the fact that he saw the interruptions and spontaneous encounters of his daily routine as being *the* essential work of evangelism. In contrast to his example, contemporary Christians are more likely to look right through the people God places in their paths each day while their imaginations run after the greater works they will plan and accomplish tomorrow. We take too lightly the admonishment that, "...the eyes of a fool are on the ends of the earth." Instead, we so easily become infatuated with where we will go, what we will do and what we will build in days to come, thereby excusing ourselves from attending to that which is before us today. This natural tendency is in contrast with two fundamental principles of spiritual power Jesus demonstrated.

The first principle is that spiritual power lies in our submission to what God is doing in the present moment: "...the Son can do nothing of himself, but what he sees the Father do; for whatever he does, the Son also does in like manner." Christianity is always a religion of the present opportunity, not the prospects and plans for tomorrow. In this respect, it is especially significant that Jesus called his disciples to, "Follow me, and I will make you fishers of men." Fishing is characterized by the 'blind' expectation of the present moment. The fisherman cannot see into the murky depths to anticipate any fish's future movement, nor can he focus on a particular fish. He pulls in his net not knowing what fish may have just swum into it of its own accord. The fisherman must have faith that his path and that of the "predestined" fish will intersect. Or he casts his hook into the dark water, being completely dependent on a fish he cannot see swallowing the bait (and the hook!) at the time of its choosing. Jesus instructed Peter accordingly, to "go to the sea, cast in a hook, and ***take the fish that comes up first.***"

When we speak of different kinds of outdoor recreation, we often mention 'hunting and fishing' in the same breath. Yet in reality, these two activities are fundamentally different in terms of the methods, perspectives, and strategies involved. A hunter is characterized by his aggressive role as a stalker, his intentional strategy to conquer the resistant will of his pre-chosen prey, and the overwhelming force of his weapon. Most significant, the hunter strategically anticipates the opportunity to take down his prey at a time and place of his own choosing. Hunting, by its very nature, is a future-orientated endeavor in that the hunter relies on his own efforts and wiles to bring about that potential opportunity for the kill that does not yet exist.

Just about everything Jesus taught about evangelism runs counter to our inclinations and assumptions as *Homo venator* (man the hunter). It would hardly be an understatement to say that most of what we commonly call 'evangelism' today resembles hunting much more than fishing. Those outside Christianity are our opponents, those whom we pursue and chase down against their wills, indeed: our prey. In response, people in today's society are keenly aware that they are being hunted; that Christians regard them as 'souls' rather than as integrated, unique individuals. We run evangelism campaigns, structure our worship services, and even enter into long-term "friendships" for the sole purpose of creating some future hunter-prey opportunity.

But while contemporary Christians pursue prospective converts with the energy and adrenalin of the hunter, Jesus is a fisherman. He stated, "...I, if I am lifted up from the earth, will draw all peoples to myself." But Christianity's greatest impediment to effective evangelism is that it doesn't really believe that people have a spiritual hunger that is drawing them to Christ of their own accord. In the New Testament, we read how Jesus continually sought out seclusion, but the crowds kept finding him. "He could not be hid." He pursued no one, yet everyone pursued him. How many of us have people "swimming" around us, gradually being attracted to Christ because they find his irresistible sensations of sight, smell and taste so appetizing? We do not naturally think of the work of evangelism in such terms. The hunter-prey model seems much more stimulating.

Understanding the different perspectives of the hunter and the fisherman can provide some valuable insights into how Christianity is to spread the gospel. For one thing, the essence of hunting is pursuit. The hunter aggressively stalks and chases after his prey. But the fisherman depends on two paths intersecting independent of his control. Once he chooses his fishing hole, his role is stationary and passive. His purpose is to be quiet, hidden and unobtrusive. He knows that he would scare the fish away if he chased them through the water trying to cast his hook directly in front of a fish's mouth. We should also consider that sight is a critical faculty of the hunter. Accurate observation of the prey is essential to success. The hunter attempts to counter every observed movement of his prey with a counter move. He is literally doing battle with his prey. However, a fisherman cannot read the mind of the fish or see what it is doing. He can only pay attention to his own business: the right location, the right fishing tackle and the right bait. Then he must patiently wait for the fish to be drawn to his hook.

The second fundamental principle is that spiritual power lies in a Christian's submissive response to that leading of the Spirit that is only given to the individual; for the Spirit only indwells and leads individuals. The imagery of the New Testament makes it abundantly clear that Christianity is to infiltrate the world through the silent, discreet and imperceptible dispersal of individual Christians into the fabric of society. A kernel of wheat only sprouts unto new life when it is buried in the ground alone, separated from all the other kernels on the sack. Salt is only palatable as a seasoning when the individual grains are scattered and dissolved on food. Yeast only leavens bread after the repeated kneading of the dough distributes the yeast throughout the whole lump. These analogies are given to teach us that the coordinated, visible campaign is not the way of the Spirit. It is not the pouring of an entire bag of seeds into one hole, or the placing of a chunk of rock salt on a plate of food or of the folding of a lump of dough only once over a batch of yeast that accomplish God's purposes.

In contrast to this principle of dispersing into the world, 21st-century Christianity is more comfortable with destination evangelism. Instead of scattering and going "into the highways," Christianity expects the world to come through *its* door. Christianity characteristically looks to the gathered body of Christ as the accumulation point for "outreach." It strives to attract inquirers to leave their own comfort zones to venture into Christianity's camp. It tries to lure the fish out of their natural habitat into an unfamiliar fish tank so it can catch them there. Instead of asking, "Where are the fish and what bait are they taking today?" it states emphatically: "Here is when and where we will fish and this is the bait we use."

Interestingly, most new Christians are more effective in their gospel outreach during their first three years than they are for the rest of their lives. There are four reasons for this:

1. They still have their pre-Christian network intact and they interact with their friends and acquaintances one-on-one. After they integrate into Christian culture, they typically stop forming new relationships outside of that environment.

2. They begin with a personal testimony: "Let me tell you what Jesus did in my life." But as they learn more about the law, they gradually shift over to a legal challenge, "Let me explain how you have broken God's law and how you can avoid suffering the penalty."

3. They initially assume dispersed outreach to be the normative pattern for spreading the gospel. However, they eventually become conditioned to

destination evangelism as they observe that this is the standard Christian protocol.

4. They gradually forget how offensive it is to a lawless culture to come into a community of the law. After they acclimatize to Christian culture, they lose perspective of what a hostile environment this is for outsiders.

Destination evangelism is especially problematic in a lawless society because the body of Christ is a community of the law, and rightly so. The assembled body of Christ celebrates God's law as its source of life, health and guidance. Its members meditate on its applications and exhort one another to apply its blessings to their lives. But expecting our relativistic, postmodern culture to blend into this community in order to hear the gospel is like mixing oil and water. I frequently hear of congregations grappling with the absence of visitors in the postmodern age. They brainstorm ways to change their worship service formats in order to make them more outsider-friendly. But the fundamental problem is not solved through using contemporary music, informal language or comfortable furniture. The basic issue is that the body of Christ is, in its essence, a community of the law. Even though our Lord never intended the gathered body to be his instrument for spreading the gospel, destination evangelism maintained a certain level of success back when Western society was a culture under the law. That society looked to Christian law for its moral guidance and the gospel could be proclaimed in that context. Today, however, a culture without the law simply will not tolerate such an environment as a medium for meeting Jesus.

You may live in a region where the rising tide of postmodernism has not yet covered the higher ground of traditional Christian culture, but where I live in the Pacific Northwest, people no longer seek out visible Christianity. They still hunger for meaning, purpose and identity, but they cannot digest our typical legal framing of the gospel. They need and want the life Jesus offers, but they will not submit to a law they believe is culturally relative and outdated. For these reasons, they do not leave the friendly environs of their march-to-your-own-drummer culture to enter into a culture of absolute law. This reality obligates 21st-century Christianity to rethink how effectively it spreads the gospel using its default "fish tank" approach.

Christians dilute the spiritual power available to them when, as the seeds, the salt grains and the leaven of the gospel, they clump together in the expectation that they can exert a greater influence through a single, coordinated strategy than they can through dispersing individually into society. This is the world's principle of influence and power, but it is the antithesis of God's plan for spreading the gospel. Such was the ambition of the architects of Babel who declared, "Come, let us build ourselves a city, and a tower whose top is in the heavens; let us make a name for ourselves, lest we be scattered abroad over the face of the whole earth." They assessed their situation accurately: either to unite in a great, common effort or to be scattered across the landscape, each one pursuing his own opportunities. But the Lord *did* scatter them because the collective excitement that accompanies our infatuation with the "great thing we can achieve together" crowds out the still, small voice that is to direct each of us in our daily way.

For this reason, Christ's body is to be a scattered people, undeniably effective in its spiritual influence, yet invisible in terms of any distinctive social, political or demographic profile. When an overwhelming army occupies a land, the resistance fighters are most effective when they strike individually without warning and immediately disappear into the local population from which they are indistinguishable in every other respect. If instead they plan coordinated attacks as larger, visible combat units, they surrender their most effective strategy and will soon be captured or destroyed. God's intent is shown in the early expansion of Christianity, that "...those who were scattered went everywhere preaching the word." The unity of the body of Christ is to be in the Spirit only. When it tries to achieve a visible unity on any other basis, it becomes an aberrant caricature of its true essence.

Christianity must therefore reject the battle of the future as a strategy that replaces our Lord's command to *go* with the expectation that a postmodern society will *come*. It is a perspective that despises the "small" things God sets before individual Christians in favor of some "tower whose top is in the heavens" that will draw in the world tomorrow. The battle of the future is an illusory diversion that devotes more attention to our meetings and programs than to that very real individual crying out to me for the next ten minutes of my time. The flesh longs to be master of the future, but Jesus calls us to be servants of the present. The promise of tomorrow's achievement entices us to chase after some imagined dramatic breakthrough, but the expectation generally exceeds the result. God's present opportunity brings with it his own strategic focus of power that our own planning will never match; for his appointments are waiting for each of us as we go about our daily affairs in a postmodern world ready to meet Jesus.

Conclusion:
The Wisdom of the Elders

My conclusion will begin with the sober recognition that, even if Christianity stopped fighting all the battles discussed in this book, a postmodern culture would certainly not welcome it back as a beloved and long-lost brother. It would be naïve to ignore the reality that there is that opposition to Christ that is spiritual in its essence; a wilful rejection of Christ's light that no reformation of Christian conduct can resolve. People do indeed love the darkness; not because Christianity has been a hard legal taskmaster, but because their deeds are evil. The proposals in this book do not envision a utopian reconciliation of Christ and culture.

Yet the Spirit is constantly drawing people to Christ; and Christian culture needs to avoid placing unnecessary snares and obstacles in the path he bids them to follow. Medical ethics is rooted in the fundamental obligation, "First, do no harm." In the same sense, 21st-century Christianity is to ensure that it does not impede those who would approach Christ. We are to make every effort to avoid Jesus' harshest condemnation of the Pharisees: "... nor do you allow those who are entering to go in." The Lord may at times deploy us to fight certain battles in our particular arenas, but Christianity's default operational strategy remains, "...as far as it depends on you, live at peace with everyone."

While the unchallenged reign of Western Christendom is ended, the memory of its pre-eminence is still fresh in our minds. We can recall that time, not so very long ago, when most people in your town and mine confessed some form of church affiliation and those who stayed home on Sunday morning actually felt guilty about it. Of those who did participate, a fair number admittedly came out of social obligation and family tradition. Today, those who attend church are there because of their personal commitment, while those who have no such commitment simply can't be bothered. Ours is an age where social institutions are not allowed to survive unless they generate an immediate return, and Christianity is no exception. People want to know what they get out of it. "What does it do for me? What does it profit?"

But regardless of what people may think of Christ, they remain his subjects. Christ *is* their rightful king and all people will confess his lordship, if not upon his first coming then most certainly at his second. So our task as Christians is not to make people subjects, for they are already his subjects. Our task is to turn rebels into loyal servants; to convince those who bristle against his law that they have a kindly monarch whose yoke is easy and refreshing. In the 21st century, rebellion against the king is strong and widespread. Many of his subjects, as we have discussed, have declared their independence and have set up their own kingdoms. They have gone off to seek their own destiny and have told Christianity to stay inside its building on the corner.

In considering Christianity's proper role in our pluralistic culture, I offer two kings of Israel: David and Rehoboam. Their lives represent contrasting responses to rebellion: that of the Spirit and that of the flesh. The very different reactions of these leaders to their own crises of authority can provide a valuable lesson for 21st-century Christianity. We will look first at the case of Rehoboam as an example of "what not to do." His story begins with the death of Solomon:

> Then Solomon rested with his fathers, and was buried in the City of David his father. And Rehoboam his son reigned in his place. And Rehoboam went to Shechem, for all Israel had gone to Shechem to make him king. So it happened, when Jeroboam the son of Nebat heard it (he was still in Egypt, for he had fled from the presence of King Solomon and had been dwelling in Egypt), that they sent and called him. Then Jeroboam and the whole assembly of Israel came and spoke to Rehoboam, saying, "Your father made our yoke heavy; now therefore, lighten the burdensome service of your father, and his heavy yoke which he put on us, and we will serve you."

The story's context is a brewing revolution against king. On Rehoboam's coronation day, there was turmoil in Israel and the new king faced a difficult situation. To begin with, the people gave the inaugural address instead of the king. They told **him** what he was going to do. The people had some legitimate complaints. Israel suffered from abuses common to many governments: mismanagement of funds, unfair taxation, an over-sized budget for the king's personal luxuries and the suspension of citizens' rights. It is often held that Rehoboam was responsible for splitting the kingdom of Israel, but this is not the whole truth. Solomon had pushed the people to their limit by imposing forced labor and this was their main grievance.

The people were fed up with this servitude and they demanded a change. The fact that they called their favorite champion, Jeroboam, back from exile shows that they were absolutely serious about rebelling against Rehoboam. They meant business! So the first thing Rehoboam encounters as king is an ultimatum from his subjects, "Get your act together and we'll serve you; otherwise we're pulling out." Rehoboam's youth had coincided with Israel's unprecedented golden age during which no dissenting voice had questioned his father's absolute supremacy. Nothing in his life experience had given him any concept of recognizing a challenge to the law. He considered this uprising not only a rebellion against him personally, but ultimately a rejection of God's non-negotiable will.

We cannot fail to note the similarity between Rehoboam and 21st-century Christianity at this point. Despite Israel's grievous injustices suffered under his father, nevertheless "…all Israel had gone to Shechem to make him king." Beneath Israel's cynicism and bitterness, there still lay buried a kernel of desire to respond to righteous leadership; and alongside it the hope that the new king might bring relief to their complaints. So they gathered at Shechem—if not expecting a positive response from Rehoboam, at least admitting that it was a possibility. Postmodern society has likewise concluded that it cannot trust Christianity to bring relief to life's pressures. People see Christianity as a burden on their lives that makes incessant demands on them, but offers little in return. How strange this attitude seems when we recall the invitation of Jesus for people to "Come to me, all who are weary and heavy laden and I will give you rest." Christianity is to be a refuge of renewal and of encouragement, yet so many of our neighbours have dug in their heels and refused to have anything to do with us. "The yoke is too hard," they complain, "And the load is too heavy. We can't keep up with everything you expect us to do and be; it's too much!" And sometimes these complaints are justified.

Rehoboam was losing authority over his people and losing it fast. He decides to seek advice tells everyone to come back in three days.

Then King Rehoboam consulted the elders who stood before his father Solomon while he still lived, and he said, "How do you advise me to answer these people?" And they spoke to him, saying, "If you will be a servant to these people today, and serve them, and answer them, and speak good words to them, then they will be your servants forever." But he rejected the advice which the elders had given him, and consulted the young men who had grown up with him, who stood before him. And he said to them, "What advice do you give? How should we answer this people who have spoken to me, saying, 'Lighten the yoke which your father put on us?'" Then the young men who had grown up with him spoke to him, saying, "Thus you should speak to this people who have spoken to you, saying, 'Your father made our yoke heavy, but you make it lighter on us'—thus you shall say to them: 'My little finger shall be thicker than my father's waist! And now, whereas my father put a heavy yoke on you, I will add to your yoke; my father chastised you with whips, but I will chastise you with scorpions!'"

When we consider the decision Rehoboam made here, we should remember that he was 41 years old. He was not a young kid born yesterday. Rehoboam knew that this was an important decision and it was no accident that he took three days to make it. The elders' advice reflected their insight that his father's policies were unsustainable. But Rehoboam knew only the pomp and splendor of Solomon's court, full of wealth, prestige and visiting dignitaries from all over the world. In the end, he did not resist the temptation to try to extend this exploitation of power into his own reign. He tried to squeeze a few more years of forced service out of Israel, but his subjects wouldn't follow him. Rehoboam misjudged the people and it cost him dearly.

So Jeroboam and all the people came to Rehoboam the third day, as the king had directed, saying, "Come back to me the third day." Then the king answered the people roughly, and rejected the advice which the elders had given him; and he spoke to them according to the advice of the young men, saying, "My father made your yoke heavy, but I will add to your yoke; my father chastised you with whips, but I will chastise you with scorpions!" So the king did not listen to the people; for the turn of events was from the Lord, that He might fulfill His word, which the Lord had spoken by Ahijah the Shilonite to Jeroboam the son of Nebat. Now when all Israel saw that the king did not listen to them, the people answered the king, saying:

"What share have we in David?

We have no inheritance in the son of Jesse.

To your tents, O Israel!

Now, see to your own house, O David!"

So Israel departed to their tents.

Rehoboam decided to play the tough guy. After all, he **was** the Lord's anointed. Surely the people would not rebel against the ancient law. But Rehoboam's hard line approach was a political disaster and he lost ten tribes in one day.

Let's go back and review the advice Rehoboam refused. When Rehoboam consulted the elders, they gave him a strategy for winning the people back. First, they counselled him to serve the people. "Rehoboam," they said, "Your father had things backward. God established this kingdom for the benefit of the people, not for the glorification of the king. The king is to be the nation's servant, not its taskmaster." Second, they advised him to speak good words to them. "Speak comfort and relief to them so they can forget their past afflictions." And finally, they gave him this promise: "if you do these things then they will be your servants forever. They will be filled with love, respect and admiration for you. The kingdom will be yours."

Rehoboam's squandered opportunity provides insight into the rebellion Christianity faces today. If we want to see people willingly return to their king, let us pay close attention to the advice Rehoboam rejected. The first point is for Christianity to be a servant of the people. The Lord has appointed us to be servants to the world. We are to give ourselves to our communities, asking nothing in return. Such an attitude is expressed clearly in Paul's testimony.

> But we were gentle among you, just as a nursing mother cherishes her own children. So, affectionately longing for you, we were well pleased to impart to you not only the gospel of God, but also our own lives, because you had become dear to us. For you remember, brethren, our labor and toil; for laboring night and day, that we might not be a burden to any of you, we preached to you the gospel of God.

Does 21st-century Christianity have this servant attitude? Or is it more concerned with imposing the burden of the law on a postmodern culture? I'm deeply concerned when I see the growing number of Christians demanding that society submit to the law. Our news headlines describe one group of Christians after another demanding that society conform to God's law. These activists have chosen the way of Rehoboam and they are reaping the same harvest: rebellion. Christ's kingdom will not be established through force labor and coercion.

Second, we are to speak good words to the people. Using New Testament terminology, we could say, "Speak the gospel rather than the law." Instead, relations between Christians and society today are poisoned with judgment. We tell them we don't like the way they live, the way they think, the way they look, the way they dress, the way they do this, the way they do that. We tell them everything we don't like about them and then we wonder why they can't hear the gospel.

So we find the elders' advice to Rehoboam to be the same as the apostles' instructions to Christians: "Serve the people and speak good words to them. If you do these things, they will serve you forever." Yet there are many Christians today who are convinced that Rehoboam's strategy is the correct one. They believe that, as society becomes more rebellious, Christianity has to meet the challenge with a bigger stick, chastising people more strongly: disciplining them not with whips, but with scorpions. But as Rehoboam's story shows, this strategy only incites greater rebellion.

His refusal to walk the path of a servant had three outcomes for Rehoboam. First, he is forced to retreat back to Jerusalem and consolidate what little remains of his kingdom. From that day forward, Rehoboam ruled only Judah and Benjamin. He only retained a small portion of the kingdom he could have had if he had treated the people properly. Second, he immediately prepares to make war against the ten rebellious tribes. Only the prophet Shemaiah's warning averts the king's folly. Rehoboam became totally confused. He regarded his own subjects as his enemies. He forgot all about his real enemies surrounding Israel's borders waiting to attack. Third, after Rehoboam retreated to Jerusalem, Jeroboam began to turn the hearts of the people away from the Lord. He forged two golden calves so that the people would not have to go to Jerusalem to worship. He created a new priesthood that was not of the tribe of Levi. He created new religious festivals, replacing those established in the law.

We see each of these principles at work today. We see a Christianity that has lost the loyalty of a people who now go elsewhere to satisfy their spiritual needs. We also see a Christianity that regards the people of the land as its enemies. Like Rehoboam, Christianity has retreated into its fortress and lives in fear of the very people God sent it to serve. In these respects, 21st-century Christianity is very much like Rehoboam—sitting alone in the city wondering what went wrong.

But there is another way.

As devastating as this situation is, rebellion is not a fatal disease that must run steadily downhill. God has provided a formula for reversing the course of rebellion and winning back a fragmented people. The Lord anointed Rehoboam's grandfather, David king over all Israel when he was just a youth. Yet it is nearly twenty years later before he is actually recognized as king and is ruling over all the tribes as one nation. The manner in which David brought these tribes together reveals a principle of restoration that is as valid today as it was three thousand years ago. This principle is found in the proverb, "When a man's ways please the Lord, He makes even his enemies to be at peace with him." Using this formula, David forged the isolated tribes of Israel into a nation. The same formula can be used today to draw scattered people back to their king.

Then all the tribes of Israel came to David at Hebron and spoke, saying, "Indeed we are your bone and your flesh. Also, in time past, when Saul was king over us, you were the one who led Israel out and brought them in; and the Lord said to you, 'You shall shepherd my people Israel, and be ruler over Israel.'"

In this passage, we witness a ceremony that was common throughout the ancient Near East; the signing of a covenant treaty. During this period in history, Canaan was divided up among numerous kings and princes. Each one controlled the largest territory that his strength would allow. The relationships between these various kings and the people of the land depended upon the treaties that that they drew up together.

There were two types of treaties these ancient kings used. The first type was a parity treaty. This was a cooperative agreement between two kings of equal power. They might agree to live in harmony, to respect each other's borders, and to join armies against a common foe if necessary. The second type is a vassal treaty. This was the treaty of the conqueror. In most cases, the vassal treaty was little more than the terms of surrender. The conquering king would gather the defeated people and dictate the terms of his occupation. He would usually demand that they visit his court periodically, that they furnish men for his army, that they pay tribute, that they offer praise and adoration to him, and that they never make an agreement with any other king.

Subjects of a vassal treaty were forced to live as an occupied nation and had very little to say about their own affairs. In ancient Canaan, the strongest king was the one who could control the greatest number of people under vassal treaties. His aim was to overpower them, intimidate them, break their will, and then use them to further his own ambitions. It may come as a surprise to learn that this is exactly what Israel offered to David. David fills the role of the king and the tribes of Israel the role of the vassal. David is assuming control over this vast people and they are obliged to be obedient to all he commands.

But there is something strange in this scene; something that would have raised the eyebrows of any Canaanite who might have witnessed this ceremony. The tribes of Israel were voluntarily coming to David to submit to a vassal treaty! Such a thing is unheard of. No one volunteers for a vassal treaty! Yet this is just how David's kingdom was established. He didn't conquer these people. He didn't threaten them. They simply walked into his city and said, "David, it's time for you to be our king." The ceremony we see here is more than a political treaty between an ancient king and some scattered tribes; it is the reconciliation of a broken society. God had called Israel out of Egypt as a nation, but for the last three hundred years they had been living as isolated tribes in the land they were to inherit together. Each was jealous of the other. They fought one another. They would gang up on one another, often for no other reason other than spite. Actually, a Canaanite would never have guessed that Israel was a nation by the way they lived. Each tribe considered the others to be enemies, and they lived up to the reputation.

We reserve our most bitter and cutting feelings not for our confessed enemies, but for our fellow citizens and neighbors. Realizing this, it is all the more amazing to consider this covenant. These people *had* been David's enemies. King Saul had led them all over the countryside in pursuit of David's blood. These tribes had schemed against each other and against their anointed king. And now, practically at the drop of a hat, all is forgotten and they are melded back into a close-knit family recognizing David's proper authority. "We are your bone and your flesh," they cried to David. In the ancient world, this was the strongest statement of unity one could utter. We could translate it like this: "We are one people and let's start living like it."

The question we need to ask is this: how did David do it? How did he reunite the house of Israel without any force, without any coercion, without any violation of these people's free choice? Well, the people themselves explain this: "You were the one who led Israel out and in." In other words, "You are the one who has been acting like a king all along." When God anointed the boy David to be king years earlier, David began to conduct himself as a king from that day forward. David really became king twice: once when God anointed him, and once when the people of Israel commissioned him. What happened in between is the formula for reconciliation. He conformed his life to the standards God requires of a servant king. He faithfully fulfilled these duties long before he received the kingdom that was rightfully his. In all circumstances, he demon-strated that he was worthy of his office. Then at the proper time, his subjects submitted to his rule of law.

I offer no prediction of the direction 21st-century society will take from here. But I do offer this testimony of hope: that in the darkest gloom of Jeroboam's apostasy, a man of God looked forward to a new day dawning, prophesying, "Behold, a child, Josiah by name, shall be born to the house of David." 'Josiah' is translated "the Lord heals." So let us be encouraged in this perplexing age of post-modern lawlessness when we see people's eyes turned in every direction but toward the true Source of light and life. And let us hold fast to the counsel of Rehoboam's elders: "If you will be a servant to these people today, and serve them, and answer them, and speak good words to them, then they will be your servants forever."

Appendix

Ten Guidelines for Communicating the Gospel to a Postmodern Culture

1. Tailor the gospel message to avoid offending a lawless culture, rather than trying to bring that culture back under the law.

2. Present the gospel as an appeal to free choice, rather than as an obligation necessary to avoid the penalty for lawbreaking.

3. Discern how lawlessness can open new opportunities for the gospel, rather than protesting the social instability it causes.

4. Proclaim *only* the gospel to the natural man, rather than trying to convince him of a law he cannot comprehend without the indwelling Spirit.

5. Rely on the Spirit to bestow the gift of faith, rather than answering postmodernism's rational objections to the law.

6. Focus on the gospel as an offer of eternal life in the age to come, rather than as a quality of life superior to postmodern alternatives.

7. Declare the gospel on its own terms, rather than reacting to postmodern culture's priorities.

8. Emphasize the gospel as being the solution for the universal problem of death, rather than the remedy for the legal problem of sin.

9. Proclaim what is true about the gospel, rather than condemning what is false about lawlessness.

10. Spread the gospel by scattering into the world, rather than trying to draw postmodern culture into the visible community of the law.

CPSIA information can be obtained at www.ICGtesting.com
Printed in the USA
LVOW080723070612

285013LV00001B/39/P